"Gabriel Rosenstock offers us a
haiku and the state of being
universe."

ION CODRESCU
Romania
Poet and haiga artist
Author-illustrator of *Something Out of Nothing: 75 Haiga*
and *Haiga: Peindre en poésie*

"A learned, imaginative and profound commentary on haiku with
many outstanding examples from around the globe,
demonstrating the form's universal appeal. Persons with little
knowledge of haiku will be captivated, while those with expertise
will feel renewed..."

GEORGE SWEDE
Canada
Co-founder of Haiku Canada
Editor of *Global Haiku: Twenty-Five Poets Worldwide*
and author of *Almost Unseen: Selected Haiku*

"Rosenstock is an excellent teacher, wise enough to realise that in
describing haiku (as in so many other things) examples are worth
a million words. He spreads before us a variegated tapestry of
haiku, by poets in all places and at all times since haiku began, as
well as from his own ingenious pen, in which 'the spirit of play
and the play of spirit are simultaneous and one'."

DAVID COBB
England
Founder of the British Haiku Society
Editor of *The Humours of Haiku* and *The British Museum Haiku*

"From the wealth of his experience, Rosenstock gives profound
advice and useful tips for the wanderer on the haiku path,
showing us how sudden enlightenment can happen in our
ordinary life."

RUTH FRANKE
Author of *Lapislazuli* and *Slipping Through Water*

"With edifying purpose, the author subtly introduces examples of haiku's apocalyptic potential of transfiguration, known in haiku and Zen as 'spiritual interpenetration' and, by so doing, offers the reader an opportunity to witness—through numinous haiku moments—the entwining of the Universal Spirit with Its Self."

JAMES W. HACKETT
Author of *The Way of Haiku, Zen Haiku and Other Zen Poems*, and *A Traveler's Haiku*

Selected titles by Gabriel Rosenstock

Where Light Begins: Haiku (Original Writing Ltd, 2012)

Fluttering their way into my head: An exploration of haiku for young people (Evertype, 2014)

Glengower: Poems for No One in Irish and English (The Onslaught Press, 2018)

Walk with Gandhi (Gandhi 150 Ireland, 2019)
with illustrations by Masood Hussain

Stillness of Crows (CreateSpace, 2018)
with artwork by Ohara Koson

Judgement Day (The Onslaught Press, 2016)
with artwork by Karl Waldmann

Bliain an Bhandé / Year of the Goddess (The Dedalus Press, 2007)

The Invisible Light (Silverstrand Press, 2012)
with landscape photography by Ron Rosenstock

Antlered Stag of Dawn (The Onslaught Press, 2015)

HAIKU ENLIGHTENMENT

HAIKU ENLIGHTENMENT

New Expanded Edition

Gabriel Rosenstock

POETRY CHAIKHANA

POETRY CHAIKHANA
www.poetry-chaikhana.com

ISBN-10: 0985467983

ISBN-13: 978-0-9854679-8-2

Sections of this book were first published separately as *Haiku Enlightenment* and *Haiku: The Gentle Art of Disappearing* in 2009 by Cambridge Scholars Publishing.

An early draft of "The Glowing Moment" was serialized in the e-journal *World Haiku Review* and another extract appeared on the websites *Poetry Chaikhana, Sacred Poetry from Around the World* and *Nonduality Salon.*

"The Universal Spirit of Issa" was first published in *Where Light Begins* (Original Writing Ltd., Dublin) in 2012. A draft of the essay also appeared on the *Poiein Kai Prattein* website.

"Haiku: The Art of Emptiness" was originally delivered as the keynote address to Haiku Canada 2015.

Some of the author's haiku have appeared in *Simply Haiku, Lá, Sirena* and in Irish in the volume *Géaga Trí Thine* (Comhar, 2006).

Nár dhéana an leabhar seo dochar d'éinne

—May this book harm no one

Haiku: One-breath poetry, traditionally seventeen syllables (5-7-5), now increasingly practised outside Japan as a free-style form, usually in three lines. It owes its impact and inspiration to a meditative flash in which he/she who experiences the haiku moment merges suddenly with perceived phenomena.

(Author's definition)

CONTENTS

THE GLOWING MOMENT

The haiku form is short, sharp, and intense because it aims to record rare glowing moments in which our life radiates rays of light.

—Ogiwara Seisensui

The dynamic pause ... In haiku, we pause for a few concentrated seconds. Not to escape from the helter-skelter – or tedium – of existence but to allow ourselves to seep into the life of things. In a dynamic way. Haiku is a gentle way of coming to a stop. A full stop!

The haiku moment refreshes us, focuses and strengthens us, encouraging us to continue on a pathless path which reveals itself uniquely to us all:

Who goes there?

> midstream halt—
> the horseman looks up
> at the falling stars

H. F. Noyes

Time has stopped for that horseman. Does he even know who he is anymore? An Indian sage, **Papaji**, says: 'Enlightenment does not happen in time. It happens when time stops.'

We will see many instances of haiku as a time-stopping device in the course of this book. Keep a sharp look out! Get ready to stop. What we view may well be minute, or minuscule, but will contain a cosmos.

—⁓—

Opening the casements of perception ... These intimate haiku-pauses ground us in the mystery of being as we open ourselves, time and time again, to new vistas and to keener insights into the living, changing universe we inhabit. They allow us to be attuned to the rhythm, colour, sound, scent, movement and stillness of life, from season to season, whoever, whatever or wherever we are.

Haiku may be used as a technique which facilitates an instant flooding of the mind. No known side-effects. More about that – much more – as we go on.

—⁓—

Though we may not take to the roads as did many of the Old Masters, haiku reminds us that we are all wanderers, in time and space. But are our eyes – and ears – truly open? Are our hearts open? Haiku is there to enrich our experience of being alive, to unfold the tapestry of living – in a flash – to bring us down to earth, where we belong:

in my hut
mice and fireflies
getting along

Issa

―――⁓⁓⁓―――

Touch and savour ... A haiku bids us to savour phenomena:

summer's end nears—
now the slow bee allows
stroking of fur

George Marsh
(*Salting the Air*, Waning Moon Press, 1997)

As it should be ... Autumn – slowing-down time for the bees! Sluggish bees can emerge in summer, too, as intoxicated as a bunch of Taoist poets. This, from **Bashō**:

this bee
how loath to emerge from deep
within the peony

Bashō

In both of these haiku we are with the bee, fully with the bee, one with the 'bee-havior' of a bee at one particular time and also, with the nature of all bees. Where the bee sucks there suck I. And then the 'I' dissolves in sweetness.

Allow yourself to be sucked into the vortex of a haiku moment. It's the only way. It is we who emerge from deep within the flower. Haiku is not some form of unfeeling, scientific observation. It is a vividly experienced exploration of a shared universe, whatever our mood!

What about the bee that totters on and makes it to see the winter? Does it not excite our compassion?

a winter bee
staggering on
for a place to die

Murakami Kijo

———

On your lips ... Many haikuists and editors of haiku journals like to read haiku aloud, remembering **Bashō's** advice: 'Repeat your verses a thousand times on your lips...' In other words, don't be flat, be sparingly sonorous.

You may utter this one as slowly as you like:

5. 4. 3.
2. 1. 0.
nude tree

Takazawa Akiko

There's quite a modern feel to those bare numbers; it's a haiku that may have been influenced by concrete poetry. We will encounter many styles and many moods in the course of *Haiku Enlightenment*, the modern and the classic.

Not all of the haiku chosen here are going to work for you: some will only truly come alive when re-read later, when your transmitters and receivers are more finely tuned.

A haiku moves us because we move in its movement and are moved by its stillness:

a crust of bread
jumps with the sparrows
round the courtyard

Dina Franin
(*Zaklonjen mjesec/The Sheltered Moon*, Croatian
Haiku Association, Samobore, 1999)

We can jump with haiku, crawl with haiku, soar with haiku, fall with haiku, and be still with haiku.

———

Soul-awakening ... The French say that we cannot know heaven if we haven't known earth.

In the autumn haiku, above, the shift of attention is to the bee. It is as if the bee slows down, for our sake, so that we can appreciate it – see it – in a new mood, a new light. Its summer of antics is all over. We are invited to experience and be part of another dynamic, one as real as that which went before and that which is yet to come. All of nature, and our own nature, comes alive.

The microscopic focus of the haiku reveals the inner order and beauty of existence, over and over again. All things come to life – including a crust of bread!

The microbiologist cannot fail to see a pattern, an underlying beauty – and endless variety – in the magnified specks he examines on the slide. So, too, with the patient, persistent haikuist – his perception of the life within and the life without becomes refined with practice, and attuned, whether the view is close-up or encompasses a panoramic vista.

We cannot tire of good haiku. It is a distillation of all that is real and pulsating in life. It is, as you will undoubtedly see, an elixir of enlightenment, always available, a grounding experience and a soul awakening.

> awakened
> > as ice bursts
> > > the water jar

Bashō

This can be read, simply, as a sound that wakes us from sleep but is it not also waking from everyday drowsy consciousness, the somnambulist state many of us are in? Haiku is a quickening of the inner life, in sympathetic correspondence to ordinary phenomena.

—◦◦◦—

The naturalness of it all ... Our last pause will be death. For the haikuist, death is another perfectly natural phenomenon, not something divorced from life or signifying its end:

> necklace of bone . . .
> ants have finished
> with the snake

Margaret Manson

'Necklace' is a lovely choice of word. But it is not an invention. It was what was seen and experienced at the time.

Many haikuists have written until their very last breath. Death-bed haiku of *haijin* (masters) – such as **Shiki** – are justly famous.

We can be in awe of anything, even our own demise. Everything is of cosmic magnitude, here and now. **F Scott Fitzgerald** ruminates in *The Great Gatsby*: 'Life is much more successfully looked at from a single window…' The haikuist would not argue with that, even the haikuist who takes to the roads.

A forensic scientist examining the bodies of certain newly departed *haijin* might wonder at an odd gesture of the hand, the hand as a claw, almost: their last act was to count syllables.

There are all sorts of death. The death of a language, the death of a culture:

> snowflakes fill
> the eye of the eagle—
> fallen totem pole

Winona Baker
(*Moss-Hung Trees*, Reflections Press, 1992)

Death has many faces. And life? Life exists in such mind-boggling diversity that it well behoves us to take it all in, in small doses – *beagán ar bheagán mar a itheann an cat an scadán*, as the Irish proverb has it, 'little by little, as the cat eats the herring':

> the hills
> release the summer clouds
> one by one by one

John Wills
(*Reed Shadows*, Black Moss Press and BLP, Canada, 1987)

Ten thousand gifts … 'Release' is a well-chosen verb. We receive all these words, these insights and illuminations as gifts, mediated by individuals, from the common pool of humanity's experience. In an average day, about how many free gifts can we expect on the haiku path? A thousand? That may be a conservative estimate. After all, **Dōgen** assures us, 'When the self withdraws, the ten thousand things advance!'

On the haiku path, the constant intrusion of the self becomes less and less persistent – moments arise that flood us with their 'itness' before our cognitive, judgemental self is given a chance to, as it were, interfere. Mentation ceases, momentarily, and while you think it is a good thing to exercise your mind, it's also a good thing to give it a rest.

—ᴧᴧᴧ—

The haiku path ... The use of 'path', above, must be qualified. **Wei Wu Wei**, a modern sage, says there is no highway or path to enlightenment: 'There is no path to Satori. It cannot be attained ... all the Masters tell us that we cannot seize Reality: it is Reality that seizes us.' True. (Whatever his father, High Sheriff of Armagh, might have made of it all!)

The chances of Reality seizing us, and sweeping away our pre-judgmental mind in the process, are increased by the dutiful practice of haiku:

> hearing
>   cockroach feet;
>   the midnight snowfall

> **Michael McClintock**
> (*Light Run*, Shiloh Press, Los Angeles, 1971)

—ᴧᴧᴧ—

Effortless attunement ... By working at haiku and by living haiku—through reading and composition and through acquiring the haiku instinct, or knack – effortless attunement is the natural and inevitable result. This ability then becomes the unfailing groundwork for sudden enlightenment. It can repeat itself, over days, over centuries. **David Burleigh** published this haiku in 1998:

> trapped inside a pot
> at the bottom of the sea
> the octopus dreams

> **David Burleigh**

Bashō wrote the following in May, 1688:

> octopus traps—
> dreams vanish under
> a summer moon

Bashō

This may be mere coincidence, or it may be evidence of the cosmic mind at work, or it could be an example of *honkadori*, allusive variation.

Mr Burleigh kindly responded to an enquiry by stating that it did, in fact, allude to **Bashō's** verse in the *Travel-Worn Satchel* but that his own haiku was inspired by the confined space of urban living.

Sudden breath of freedom ... Confined no more! Each successful haiku is a breath of freedom. The seventeen-syllable, traditional form was adjudged to be a breath span. And, just as **Keats** said that poetry should come as naturally as foliage to a tree, or not at all, so we say that haiku is an exhalation, a breath of freedom, of exultation, a sigh.

You may polish your haiku, once it has come to you, or come through you. Honing the shape, changing the line order, improving the choice of words, or the rhythm or punctuation – these are the wrapping on the gift. But there need be nothing laborious about the strange appearance of the first draft. 'Haiku should be written as swiftly as a woodcutter fells a tree or a swordsman leaps at a dangerous enemy.' So said **Bashō**, born into an impoverished samurai clan. This suddenness, indeed, is what allows for the possibility of enlightenment. No time to think!

—〜〜—

T
H
I
N
K

They say that characters were engraved on the bathing tub of King Tching Thang to this effect: 'Renew thyself completely each day; do it again, and again, and forever again.' I can understand that.

— **Thoreau**, *Walden*

A
B
O
U
T

I
T

It is a plunge ... On the way of haiku, we cannot possibly know what next will be revealed. We are not soothsayers. Nor do we dabble in magic. What will be the next haiku moment? Anticipation is foolish. Each moment is as unique as your fingerprints, your iris, each second as fleeting as your breath. And a haiku moment can happen at any time. But it will not happen without you. You must be there for it to happen. You must be there, before you disappear. It takes two to haiku, you and the witnessed phenomenon in a unifying embrace.

It can occur in such an intense, pure form that it appears to have happened without you. That brief, piercing insight, that moment of haiku enlightenment, strips you of the thousand and one items that are the jigsaw of your ego, the patchwork of your identity. Then we're simply jumbled back again into the duality of the world, its conflicts, routines and distractions. But we know that another pure surprise waits around the corner, whatever it may be. The wellsprings of the haiku moment are infinite, bottomless, inexhaustible.

The glimpse ... The haiku moment can occur in a glimpse. A glimpse of the beloved. The glowing, two-way, time-stopping intensity of that glimpse!

To put the words of a contemporary Western sage, **Gangaji**, to our own uses here: 'The glimpse and the surrender into that glimpse, the surrender of the mind into what is glimpsed, gives rise to everything we are seeking...' (*Gangaji News*, June 11, 2003)

Rebirth in the pure self ... On the haiku path, you can dissolve and change into your purer self. Many haiku poets take a nom de plume or *haigo*. It's a bit like Saul becoming Paul, is it not? The avant-garde haikuist **Ban'ya Natsuishi** explains his new name, a name which he has carried for over quarter of a century. *Ban* is 'fit' and *ya* is 'arrow'. So, his identity is now shaped by the purpose and the skill of fitting an arrow to a bowstring. Cool! This coolness is balanced by the passion he has for haiku. *Natsu* means 'summer' and *ishi* means 'stone'. Hot!

The first entry in *Haiku, This Other World*, by **Richard Wright**, reads as follows:

I am nobody:
A red sinking autumn sun
Took my name away

Richard Wright

This is profoundly moving, coming as it does from a writer passionately concerned with questions of identity and negritude and for whom a harsh Mississippi boyhood could so easily have estranged him from the bountifulness and beauty of the earth.

—◦◦◦—

Surprise of unity ... Everything about our existence seems fractured from the time our umbilical cord is cut. Haiku offers us a direct route towards unity. It is put well by **Jonathan Clemens** in *The Moon in the Pines* (Frances Lincoln Limited, 2000):

> 'Haiku seeks, in a handful of words, to crystallise an instant in all its fullness, encouraging through the experience of the moment the union of the reader with all existence. The reader side-steps conventional perception, startled into a momentary but full understanding of the poet's experience. By locking reader and poet into the same reality, haiku helps us perceive the ultimate unity of all realities...'

Alive alive-o! The aliveness of haiku is one of its most remarkable gifts. Did not **Thomas Traherne** say that you will not be able to enjoy the world as you should 'until the sea itself floweth in your veins...':

whatever I pick up
is alive—
ebbing tide

Chiyo-ni

Yes, more and more free gifts! Good haiku fulfils the Emersonian dictum, every time: **Emerson** said that poetry must be as new as foam and as old as rock.

—◦◦◦—

bhfuil áit níos fearr ann
ná anseo anois—
corra bána ar eitilt

is there a better place
than here and now—
white herons in flight

よりよき処ありや
ここより今より —
白鷺の飛ぶ

(Mariko Sumikura)

nae brawer place
nor here'n nou -
fite herns in flicht

(John McDonald)

Newness and aliveness ... Haiku practice leads to a feeling of newness and aliveness. No, it's more than a feeling. It is an actual, existential discovery of newness. In all things. Haiku is a vehicle for regeneration.

Can one feel enlightenment? Let us be a little inscrutable about this and say that feelings may or may not be part of the experience. Sudden enlightenment is liberation – from feelings, from cognition. *Webster's Third New International Dictionary* lists enlightenment as 'the state of being in harmony with the laws of the universe' (Taoism) and also 'the realisation of ultimate universal truth' (Buddhism). Haiku practise is not at variance with these goals. Indeed, the haiku way is the goal itself, not a path to something else.

And here is a lovely Christian manifestation of haiku truth:

> April snow—
> the lightness of the Host
> in my hand
>
> **Adele Kenny**
> (*Frogpond*, No. 3, 1998)

A metaphysical gift! This particular haikuist is a member of the Secular Franciscan order and believes that writing haiku 'means using words reverently to express the sacredness of God's universe – in moments of isolation, in moments of communion – alone and yet united with the Creator and with all creation...'(*ibid.*).

The mood of haiku changes, from moments of isolation to moments of intense communion. 'Achieve enlightenment, then return to this world of ordinary humanity...' Thus spoke **Bashō**. Indeed, seeing into the life of things seemed to be enough for **Bashō** as *satori*-seeking in itself may not be the most enlightening of pursuits:

> how sublime!
> one who finds no enlightenment
> in the lightning flash
>
> **Bashō**

And this creation, this created world that we speak of, is everything, not just mountains, rivers and deserts:

I sleep… I wake…
the bed is vast
with none to share

Chiyo-ni

—*∿*—

Creation is presence – and absence too …

Autumn – looking at the moon
no child
on my knee

Onitsura

the willow is felled—
kingfishers come
no more

Shiki

It is meeting, and parting …

I've just got to know
the scarecrow
and now we part

Izen

It is music older than time … It is not any one thing, but many things
together in strange harmonic fusion which the haikuist intuits, 'the music of
things that happen', as we read in classical Irish lore:

night vanishes
behind the peaks—
bellowing deer

Kyokusi

It is fierce ...

> an autumn squall
> topples the eagle
> over the cliff edge

Ryōta

It is gentle ...

> mist among grasses,
> silent rain,
> evening calm

Buson

It is holy ...

> his hands together—
> frog
> recites a poem

Sokan

It is empty and full ...

This misty morning—
> adrift on the high water
> an empty canoe

O Mabson Southard
*(Deep Shade, Flickering Sunlight: Selected
Haiku of O Mabson Southard*, 2004)

It can be found everywhere ... We should note what **Mircea Eliade** says
in his Diary:

'In his book, Zen in Japanese Art, Hasumi noticed that art represents
the way to the Absolute. Tea ceremony, as well as the other "ways"
(dō) – painting, poetry, ikebana, calligraphy, archery – form a spiritual
technique, as its aim is obtaining "the Nirvana experience" in everyday
life.'

16

Yes, haiku is part of everyday life. Nothing, apart from a little notebook, distinguishes the haikuist from anybody else you may pass on the street. He or she may have had a Nirvana experience that morning – or is about to have one now, this instant! But no alarms or fireworks are going off; there is nothing untoward. Everything is normal.

Haiku highwayman ... He will stop us again and again on the road, take our clothes, our money, our watch, our identity papers, leaving us dumbfounded, looking around like a naked waif. He gives us time to wonder at our nakedness, at the universe, to look at the sky, at the moon, for the first time.

Then he throws everything back at us again, laughingly. And as we pick ourselves together, we know the world has changed. We smile. We, too, have changed.

Yes, it can be like that. Generally speaking, however, the Nirvana experience can be as perfectly ordinary as opening or closing one's umbrella, as undramatic as stepping over a snail on a footpath.

The Heraclitean truth ... 'You never step into the same river twice,' is a truth lived each day by the haikuist, one that is essential to the aesthetics of haiku consciousness:

> autumn wind—
> letters emerge one by one
> on the wet tombstone

> **Yamazaki Hisao**

On one level, any unexpected revelation, however ordinary, can be the stuff of enlightenment. On another level, our readiness to absorb the revelation, our ability to be struck by some 'epiphany' (as **James Joyce** used the word) becomes the real stuff of enlightenment.

There are no steps to enlightenment. Steps lead to further steps and so on. There is only the laughing plunge, the sober awakening. No ashram or yoga needed here, no prayer or mediation. The garden is your ashram, the public park, the highway – and the haiku is your prayer, your meditation.

You can make the plunge any hour of the day or night. You won't hear the splash, but the ripples are real. They will change you and the world.

—◁◁◁—

Instant enlightenment ... Many haikuists, but not all, are familiar with Zen which got its first mention in the West from **Madame Blavatsky** and its first exposition in 1927 by **D. T. Suzuki**. 'Familiar' is not the best word, as part of the Zen thing is the shock of the familiar seen in unfamiliar light, and vice versa. **Caroline Gourlay**, one-time editor of *Blithe Spirit*, Journal of the British Haiku Society, recalls how deeply impressed she was with these lines found in *The World of Zen*, an anthology edited by **Nancy Wilson Ross**:

> 'The wild geese do not intend to cast their reflection.
> The water has no mind to receive their image…'

Haiku happens in this world of daily miracles and is a perfect prism through which Nature herself enlightens us. But, instant enlightenment? Surely not! How many people have spent their lives – many lives – in such a quest! This book is a plea to lower your sights, somewhat, to focus your vision. Thousands set themselves such an impossible task that they inevitably lose sight of their goal, blaming themselves needlessly.

This little book, containing haiku by practitioners from all over the world, ancient and new – and the new are as ancient as the ancient are new – this book will open up a universal path which you may have been walking already, as it happens, without knowing it! Page after page, you will notice what little adjustment is needed – if any – to our antenna in order to receive frequent sprinklings of enlightenment, leading to an acquired receptivity which allows us to be sprinkled and purified more and more – until nothing is left in the world which is not truly, in itself, a vehicle for liberation.

—◁◁◁—

Freedom now ... One is reminded, in this regard, of the students of Ayurveda in ancient India. Three of them were instructed to go out into the forest and return with something of no medicinal value whatsoever. Two returned with what they thought to be seemingly useless objects; the third was slow to return and when he did he was empty-handed for he had searched high and low and failed to find any blessed thing that did not contain some medicinal value.

The haikuist is that blessed third student – always looking, not with bleary-eyed concentration, not merely looking but intuiting the molecules of liberating grace.

Our tendency towards self-aggrandisement will diminish the more delicately we respond to the spirit of haiku, until it is with a smile of recognition that we realise why **Yataro Kobayashi** changed his name to **Issa**, meaning a single bubble in a teacup – gone before you have raised the cup to your lips.

—*wv*—

Grandeur in little things ...

> old pear tree
> now laden only with
> raindrops

Philip D. Noble

This haiku (from the 1998 Mainichi Haiku Contest) is not concerned with some grand, amorphous or Romantic concept of Nature. In Haiku, we discover, see and breathe, for a moment, those interstices, those fleeting moments of reality which are as substantial or as insubstantial as a rock, as ourselves.

The haiku bears witness to the non-judgemental aspect of our humanity, that instinct for self-expression which drove the ancients to illuminate their caves with spectacular representations of those animals with which they shared this earth, long before philosophy, theology and economics became possible. An instinct to share in the life of things, partake in the life of things – their simple grandeur – and be blessed by them, an instinct there since the dawn of consciousness.

—*wv*—

Primitive enlightenment ... Yes, haiku enlightenment is a primitive form of enlightenment, tempered by a sensitivity that comes with practising the form. And history shows us that sensitivity is not a recent acquirement. The Chauvet cave in France was painted 31,000 years ago! **Freud**, in *The Ego and the Id* (1927), reminds us that thinking in pictures is immensely older than thinking in words:

wintry river in spate—
a dog's forsaken
carcass

Buson

Many in the West – and, now, increasingly elsewhere – live in a cosseted, sanitized, cosmeticized environment. Haiku allows us to experience the shock of primal experience so that something flows within us again, by virtue of haiku-seeing:

winter stars
a wild goose tucks its head
under a wing

Kirsty Karkow

Haiku-seeing can also be a different way of seeing the world:

broken sky
a single pony
keeps the field from straying

John W. Sexton
(*Shadows Bloom*, Doghouse 2004)

There is magic here! Haiku that lack magic and mystery are not really haiku at all. They may conform to the structure and appearance of haiku but that is not enough. They must be capable of transforming writer and reader alike.

The above haiku is almost a prayer. Sexton is in awe of nature. Not in the sense of an open-mouthed village idiot frightened by the workings of nature. On the contrary. There is a sensitivity and intelligence at work here which is engaged in a sacramental embrace of natural phenomena. Written in Kerry, in the south of Ireland, some places seem to be blessed with full haiku potential. Kerry is where you will find the Paps of Danu, two breast-like mountains which, when kissed by sunlight, can induce ecstasy in the beholder and in the goddess herself.

There are those who say, 'Nature? Irrelevant!' We reply in the words of **Reiner Kunze**: 'Nature is what is forever valid, and also retains validity in the poetic image, elevating it to universality.' ('In Time of Need', *A Conversation about Poetry, Resistance & Exile*, Reiner Kunze, Mireille Gansel, Libris, 2006)

PAUSE

Please pause.
This is not a roller coaster!

Have a cup of tea or a favourite tipple.

Take a walk.
Observe.
Absorb.

Or put on some music. Have a look at the fellow with a straw box on his head on YouTube, playing the *shakuhachi* flute.

Or perhaps it's time to turn the pages back?

Did something strike you?
Why?

Or simply breathe.
Or stare into nothingness!

Find silence.

Nothing nurtures the spirit more than silence.
When you return, there will be many more delightful haiku to enjoy.
The ways to haiku enlightenment will be presented to you, sometimes illustrating the same point from slightly different angles.
Don't get smothered in an avalanche of words.
Try taking a pause before and after each haiku and before and after each section of this book.

Stabilization of haiku enlightenment ... You're back!

Welcome!
How's it going?
Where were we?
Where are we?
In haiku world.
In the real world.
Is it the real world?
That is what we are going to determine.

The writing of haiku and the sharing of haiku is a perfectly selfless act. Utterly selfless. As such, it conforms to the teachings of the Gita: 'Those who work selfishly for results are miserable.'

We are all of us capable of writing hundreds – even thousands – of haiku. Each true haiku momentarily destroys the false self and its illusory sense of self-importance; the false self fights back, of course, thinking it (and only it) is real – only to be bombarded once more with the force of a haiku moment of pure consciousness. Eventually, the long-suffering divided self yields to the grace of Oneness and the haikuist's enlightenment becomes stabilized.

––––––

The enigmatic sage, **Wei Wu Wei**, proposes the following formula: 'The Saint is a man who disciplines his ego. The Sage is a man who rids himself of his ego.' (*Fingers Pointing Towards the Moon*, Sentient Publications, 2003).

We do not discipline the ego with haiku. We slough it off, it sloughs itself off. Ego has no time or space in which to assert itself within the sanctum of the haiku moment.

It might take you long arduous years and a hair-shirt to become a saint. You are only a breath away from being a sage. Not even that. You are already a sage. It's just that you don't know it. While this concept may come as a surprise to you, it is a commonplace in the library of world wisdom. So, don't worry. Just write haiku. Everything else will take care of itself.

––––––

T
H
I
N
K

When you express gentleness and precision in your environment, then real brilliance and power can descend onto that situation. If you try to manufacture that presence out of your own ego, it will never happen. You cannot own the power and the magic of this world. It is always available, but it does not belong to anyone.

— **Chögyam Trungpa**

A
B
O
U
T

I
T

The poetics of haiku . . . has always meant walking out into nature and having the natural world move through me . . .

— **Wally Swist**

There are none so blind ... It was **Ruskin** (1819-1900) who, perhaps, first saw the blindness inflicted on us by the modern world. Addressing his students at the Working Men's College he is reported as having said: 'Now, remember, gentlemen, that I have not been trying to teach you to draw, only to see.'

He then went on to describe two men going through a market. One emerges none the wiser. The other 'notices a bit of parsley hanging over the edge of a butter-woman's basket.' Had he known about haiku, **Ruskin** might have said, 'And there, gentlemen, is the haiku moment ... the birth of a haiku. In the act of seeing.'

And after that? What comes then? Well...

> Morning. The haiku
> are writing
> themselves

Tom McGrath
(*Atoms of Delight: an anthology of Scottish haiku and short poems*,
Ed. **Alec Finlay**, Morning Star Publications, 2000).

Seeing with the heart ... the spirit ... It is more than seeing with the eye. We read in the preface to the tenth-century royal collection of poems, *Kokinshu*: 'The poetry of Japan takes the human heart as seed and flourishes in the countless leaves of words...'

As a literary device, haiku has endless sophistication. But literature is not our main concern here. We are talking first and foremost about a delightful awareness-tool:

> nothing but pilgrims' staffs
> passing through—
> summer fields

Ishu

Followers of the mystic traditions of East and West, devotees of **Krishnamurti** (whether the gentle **J.** or the mind-blasting **U. G.**), **Osho**, **Meister Eckhart** or **Rumi**, etc., can and should follow the haiku path.

This path does not contradict Christianity, Buddhism, Hinduism, Islam, Judaism, nor can it in any way detract from the core of these or any other religions. This path is not a religion or a cult, though some neo-pagans and pantheists may be more initially attracted to it than, let us say, fundamentalists of the kill-joy variety.

Haiku can be pleasurably pursued by atheist, sceptic and believer alike. It can adapt to any language, any culture. Someone once asked the Zen teacher, **Toni Packer**, 'Can a leaf swirling to the ground be my teacher?' Her answer is what every haikuist should know. 'Yes! Of course! This instant of seeing is the timeless teacher, the leaves are just what they are…'

> summer drought—
> the dazzling stars
> all become pale

Marijan Cekolj

summer fog
moonlight blowing
from tree to tree—

Dave Sutter

—*vvv*—

Opening the channels of energy … And when you enter the haiku moment, in a flash, whether you lose yourself or whether you still retain a notion of the "I", one thing is certain – there occurs a blissful, and also a sobering new energy which comes from letting go.

Some traditional musicians experience this, as do certain jazz musicians, slipping into an extemporising mode and momentarily entering a universe in which normal constraints are shattered. After all, if we look at the word 'extemporise', does it not mean to be outside of time? Enter!

This fusion of energies is our birthright, ecstatically described by the unorthodox Zen Master, **Ikkyu Sojun** (1394 – 1481) in his miniscule poems:

> I'm in it everywhere
> what a miracle trees lakes clouds even dust

Ikkyu
(*Ikkyu: Crow with no Mouth*, versions by **Stephen Berg**,
Copper Canyon Press, 2000)

—*vvv*—

You should also know that what may not be happening is as important as what may appear to be happening:

> going nowhere
>   during the air-raid alarm—
>   a scarecrow

Aleksandar Pavic
(*A Scarecrow in the Snow*, Moment Book, Novi Sad, 2000)

—◌◌◌—

The configuration of three lines and – initially, before trying free-style haiku – seventeen syllables, 5-7-5, will in itself be a discipline to help you to see, capture and structure the haiku moment, to recognise it, instantly, as it occurs. It occurs in an instant! You may have to wait for it, though:

> watching the pond still
>   finding
>   new depths

Eric I. Houck, Jnr
(*In Sparrow*, Croatian Haiku Association, 1999-2000)

Haiku lets go of concepts, of thoughts, of presuppositions, of opinions, prejudices and all the burden of the mind:

> in spring waters
>   a certain thought
>   floated away

Sekishi Takagi

—◌◌◌—

Letting go … Of course, haiku does not erase or eliminate any of those elements that make up our consciousness or personality traits. On the contrary, it brings consciousness to the fore – by letting go.

We can bring our moods with us into the haiku world, or allow our mood to be coloured by our surroundings, the weather, the season, the interpenetrating sounds, odours, textures, light and shade.

Enter into them all, at once! Our natural reaction to all these elements is much truer than anything we might fantasise about. And if memory is part of living in the witnessing present, then memory, too, can feature in a haiku:

Der Wintermond stand
heute über Hesses Grab.
Weite Erinn'rung

The winter moon
over Hesse's grave—
faraway memories…

Günter Klinge
(*Sparrow*, 1999 – 2000)

True sensitivity to the present does not erase the past; far from it. The present may be enriched by a conscious or unconscious invoking of the past. From Hawaii:

evening sun
shadows line
the old school yard

Gail H. Goto

—∿∿—

A time for every purpose under heaven … Some of the above haiku allude to seasons. Seasonal allusion was, until recently, a necessary ingredient in Japanese haiku. A word that places you in a particular season is called *kigo*.

Thus the skylark or the activity of tea-picking are associated, in Japan, with spring. Fireflies are an indication of summer, deer and mushrooms signify autumn, the eagle and the pine belong essentially to winter.

But you needn't be aware of the thousands of indicators that have traditional seasonal echoes. Find your own. No need to be more Japanese than the Japanese themselves. No, we can – and must – be ourselves first before losing the self, sacrificing the self, momentarily, in haiku.

It is quite enough that we absorb the spirit of haiku from reading the best of the old and new and sharpen our technique so that it fulfils the promise offered here in all sincerity – haiku enlightenment!

Right here and now ... The German-Jewish poet, **Heinrich Heine,** claimed that the best songs of summer are composed in front of a roaring fire in winter; what may be true of poetry is not true for haiku. Generally speaking, those haiku dealing with a particular season are written in that season, are experienced in that season and belong to that season. In this respect, haiku enlightenment is a very grounding experience, in place and in time. Sand-castles in the sky? A noble occupation, but don't use haiku if that's your game. There is absolutely no need to fantasise.

The haiku moment is as exactly as it should be, right here and now, its contours awaiting you in the emptiness of a timeless glimpse. The task is not to extract its ingredients, somehow, but to become part of its molecular structure, its essence, colour, sound, sharing its invisible nature, melding into that moment which is the summation of all of existence now, the core of creation.

—————

Stop! Listen ... This is the haiku's time and place, no other. Its expression may, indeed, be coloured by past fantasies and experiences but its realm is the eternal now.

Jung's idea of synchronicity, the drawing of Tarot cards, astrological configuration, the law of universal correspondence ... as above so below ... some of these notions may be connected to the haiku moment. Let us live with these mysteries.

> I stop to listen;
> the cricket
> has done the same

Arizona Zipper
(*A Pale Leaf,* New York, 1981)

Haiku will change your behaviour patterns! You will hear more and see more than ever before. You are noticing much more because you have become more aware of significance.

after Christmas
a flock of sparrows
in the unsold trees

Dee Evetts
(*Endgrain*, Red Moon Press, 1997)

Haiku will change the way you see – how you see and what you see.

In the haiku moment, time is frozen, melding, suspended, yet bursting with life. We are primordial once again, innocent, all senses alive, truly at one with our surroundings, truly human, strong and vulnerable, in a state of grace:

looking together
across the frozen lake
the heron and I

Jan van den Pol

—*∿∿*—

Openness to openness … Haiku encounters the truth in an open, natural state of mind and that openness and humility is rewarded by enlightenment. 'Deep answereth unto deep, love respondeth unto love…' and, let us add, openness to openness. Because enlightenment is an opening up to see the light.

The haikuist is a seer. Even be he blind, the haikuist still sees. It is the spirit that sees.

—*∿∿*—

Reward of trust … While often seeming to concentrate on – or probe – that which is almost imperceptible, haiku is a flowering, an opening up to the world and this trust is rewarded from day to day.

The haiku is a returning to the world, a returning to reality, a 'teshuva', as John the Baptist said, and wrongly translated as 'repent'. Let us relish the wisdom in the following:

"To return to things themselves is to return to that world which precedes knowledge, of which knowledge always, and in relation to which every scientific schematisation is an abstract and derivative sign-language, as is geography in relation to the countryside in which we have learnt beforehand what a forest, a prairie or a river is…"

— **Maurice Merleau-Ponty** (*Phenomenology of Perception*, Humanities Press, 1962)

—⁓⁓—

What is the shape of today? Does that sound like a riddle, a *koan*? Let's see. So … you think you know what a mountain looks like, what a summer stream sounds like? Or is it merely an idea of a mountain or a stream that you are entertaining? **Seishi** (1901 –1994) transmits the genuine haiku experience beautifully:

> dunes in a bitter wind—
> the shape they take on,
>   the shapes of today . . .

Seishi

Shapes of emptiness … In our bustling, noise-polluted world, chock-full of garish images, the haiku way of living alludes to the void, the throbbing silence at the heart of it all; deep, inviolable stillness in ourselves. **Robert Bebek**, the Croatian *haijin*, gave the title *Oblici Praznine/The Shapes of Emptiness* to his highly distinguished second book:

> warming even
> an empty room, a
> beam of morning sun

Robert Bebek

—⁓⁓—

one by one
thoughts slip away . . .
morning sky

smaointe ag imeacht
ina gceann is ina gceann . . .
spéir na maidine

Enlightenment pool ... As the initiate becomes accustomed to reading, writing and recognising good, sublime haiku, there arises an intimate sharing of the haiku moments of others. Enlightenment becomes pooled.

sickle moon—

reaping

emptiness

GR

—⁓—

T
H
I
N
K

Between two thoughts there is an interval of no thought. That interval is the Self, the Atman. It is pure awareness.

— *Jnana Vashistha*

A
B
O
U
T

I
T

Gifts and works ... "We should learn to see God in all gifts and works," said **Meister Eckhart**, "neither resting content with anything nor becoming attached to anything..." This means that we mustn't become too attached to haiku!

How rich the haiku harvest is once we become poor in spirit. Walk this lonely, companionable way with us:

wet west Muskerry—
        moonlight
                drying the clothes

Seán Mac Mathúna

Yes, that is a little bit crazy. But let's not forget that haiku was once dubbed *kyōku*, crazy verse! The rational mind – given that it might be able to compose such a haiku – would have rejected it instantly, depositing it deep in the waste-paper basket, in the hope that no neighbour or colleague might fish it out. But there is nothing crazy about it, or sane, nothing good, nothing bad about it, nothing right or wrong about it. It is simply what it is.

Consider, now, the words of **Chuang Tzu**: "When we look at things in the light of Tao, nothing is best, nothing is worst. Each thing, seen in its own light, stands out in its own way."

Learning selfhood ... The magic of the **Mac Mathúna** haiku is that it appears to happen without the interference of human agency. But it only appears that way. The human imagination is actively at work, transforming one reality into another. The human spirit is at work, language is at work, as effortlessly as the trained Inuit shaman travels silently to the moon.

"Learning the way of enlightenment is learning selfhood.
Learning selfhood is forgetting oneself.
Forgetting oneself is being enlightened by all things..."

— **Dōgen** (Quoted in the Introduction to *Kensho, The Heart of Zen* by Thomas Cleary, Shambhala, 1997).

        ancient temple—
        the snake sloughs off
        his worldly scales

Issa

Forgetting oneself is not a retreat to some Elysian passivity! It is not absent-mindedness. If you are competitive in sports or in business, 'forgetting oneself' is the key to spontaneous action and initiative. Who has ever crossed the winning line in a hundred metre dash, or hit the bull's eye in a game of darts, by thinking of himself? Or for that matter, who has ever truly loved another by thinking of himself?

When you are old and grey ... and nodding by the fire... Traditional societies respected their elders. Some even worshipped them. The concept of ageism, the neglect of the elderly, prejudice against the elderly – are these the bitter harvest of a youth culture which came to the fore in the 1960s, or products of a society which evaluates our usefulness as mere worker-bees?

The haikuist sees beauty in the aged person – or thing – in the gnarled:

> dangerous pavements,
> but I face the ice this year
> with my father's stick

> **Seamus Heaney**

> grandma and grandpa
> side by side on the couch—
> wearing each other's glasses

> **Lee Gurga**

This, too, will pass ... Estrangement, alienation, displacement, these are some of the pathologies of the 21st century. But living haiku does not suffer estrangement. In joy or in wistfulness, in sadness, pain, or in sorrow, the haikuist is at one with friends, family, strangers, lizards, the stars above, seeing the mutability and vulnerability of all beings, and of ourselves. This oneness is an all-redeeming illumination. This oneness bestows extraordinary vision and a compatibility with all life forms. Nothing will ever be the same again. (Nothing was ever the same; nothing is ever what it seems):

August heat
the old orange cat sits up and licks
the sun from its tail

George Swede
(*Almost Unseen, Selected Haiku of George Swede*, Brooks Books, 2000)

―――∾∿∾―――

Why furry, feathery creatures are our relations ... Diane Wolkstein,
writing in the influential journal Parabola, shares with us the wisdom of the
oral tradition of the now extinct Karraru People from Australia. It could be
the Haiku Gospel:

> 'All around you are your relations – the crawling, moving, feathery,
> and furry creatures – the water, the grass, the hills, and the wind. This
> is their place. Now it is your place, too. Where you were born is your
> Dreaming. You must always take care of that piece of land... Care for
> the land for your grandmothers and grandfathers, as well as for your
> grandchildren. I travelled every step of the earth and it is alive...'

Which one of us would not like to feel the truth of all that deep within
ourselves and to know it actively in our lives! With haiku we can and we
do. What? We think like that? Proclaim feathery, furry creatures to be our
relations? Hmm... Do we? Can we? Should we? **Thomas Berry**, also
writing for *Parabola*, challenges our scepticism and insists that, 'The outer
world is necessary for the inner world. The greatest and deepest tragedy in
losing the splendour of the outer world is that we will always have an inner
demand for it.' Without the natural world, he claims, 'our integral spiritual
development can never take place.'

―――∾∿∾―――

Odour of chimpanzee ... Many non-haikuists can show us, in the
immediacy of their engagement with Nature, what joy awaits us on the
haiku path. Environmentalist and primate specialist **Jane Goodall** is a fine
witness to these experiences: '... the air was filled with a feathered
symphony, the evensong of birds...' This is a typical, passive activity
among haikuists, hearing birdsong. With time, the ability to listen increases
naturally and the concomitant pleasure. **Goodall** continues: 'I heard new
frequencies in their music and also in the singing insects' voices – notes so
high and sweet I was amazed.' This is what can happen on the haiku path. It
is not magical or exceptional in any way. It is perfectly natural. And she
says: 'Never had I been so intensely aware of the shape, the colour of
individual leaves, the varied patterns of the veins that made each one

unique. Scents were clear as well, easily identifiable: fermenting, overripe fruit; waterlogged earth; cold, wet bark, the damp odour of chimpanzee hair...' (*Reason for Hope: A Spiritual Journey*, Warner, 2000).

—⟋⟍⟋⟍⟋—

The two ways are one ... Haiku can encompass the two classical approaches of the *via negativa* and the *via positiva* – the choice is yours. One can have a foot in both camps!

In the *via negativa* we favour solitude and contemplation and the image may be doleful, a crow or a sewer rat. In the *via positiva* we are outgoing, comprehensive, all-embracing, merging with the whole and our images may be colourful parrots at sunrise!

—⟋⟍⟋⟍⟋—

Constant renewal ... Crafts people and artists in all disciplines go to Nature, not to copy Nature, but to find something new:

'Nature is the eternal creator where each art comes to be renewed, where the eye of every thinker and artist reads a different poem...'

— **Emile Gallé** (Quoted in *Masterworks of Louis Comfort Tiffany*, Duncan, Eidelberg, Harris, Thames and Hudson, 1998).

The haiku path reconnects us. To everything. Not just, say, to the full moon. That would be too easy. No, to the moon in all its phases, life in all its phases:

Fourteenth day moon—
the distant cry of a child
somehow familiar

Yoshiko Yoshino

(*Tsuru*, translated by Lee Gurga and Emiko Miyashita, Deep North Press, 2001)

Connecting us to haiku!

I rub my nose
over and over – how skilful
are Kyoshi's haiku

Yoshiko Yoshino
(*ibid.*)

—⁓—

From certainties to ambiguities … Our aim here is not to furnish a set of dogmatic principles or practises together with a five-year guaranteed Certificate of Enlightenment. The haiku (and its related, lighter form, the *senryu*) is not at all afraid of the foibles and ambiguities which are an inevitable consequence of living life boldly and to the full:

after the divorce
she sleeps on his side
of the bed

Stuart Quine

Does **Quine's** *senryu* (named after **Karai Senryu**, 1718-1790) mean that she misses him, partakes as it were of his absent warmth? Or might it mean that she preferred his side of the bed and now has the freedom to enjoy it?

The way of haiku welcomes ambiguities, the shadows and blurs of life, the spoors of existence, be they vivid or faint:

cloud shadows
on silent cliffs
where condors nested

Jerry Kilbride

An ornithologist? No, an Irish-American bar-man in San Francisco. A veteran of the Korean War. A haikuist! Now diseased.

after months of rain
surprised
by my shadow

Ken Jones

38

The Japanese term *ada* means that mood, that style which suggests we can be surprised. Few qualities are more treasured by great achievers in life, be they artists or scientists, philosophers or gardeners. By practising and living haiku, we recover the lost innocence of childhood and *ada* colours the way we view the world anew.

—*∾*—

Tread softly ... Enlightenment is not omniscience! Mystery remains at the heart of creation. Fragility, too:

> *omokage ya*
> *oba hitori naku*
> *tsuki no tomo*

> the old woman's face—
> none stands by her now
> but the moon

Bashō

Walk this path, this compassionate path, not with strident certainty; walk the haiku path, tread softly.

—*∾*—

Issa wrote the following haiku on the death of his daughter, Sato-jo. She was the poet's second of four children to die:

> this world of dew—
> dew, yes, to be sure
> yes, but—

Issa

Worth repeating ... In haiku, some things are worth repeating. Beating one's breast once is not always enough:

riding the waves
riding those waves,
the cormorant's loneliness

Seishi

Had **Seishi** said, 'the lonely cormorant', the effect would be almost trite and sentimental. But 'the cormorant's loneliness' carries with it every aching heart in creation, bobbing on the ocean of life.

———

Face to face ... Haiku is about living, about life and death. It is about being intensely alive. We engage with life, confront demons; with haiku, there is nothing to shirk.

Luke-warm haiku will enlighten nobody. To simply espouse a philosophical, ethical or religious creed that has compassion at its heart is next to useless if the body-mind is not alert to the occasions that elicit and arouse our compassion. Thus, the haiku path triggers the salvation mechanism within us all – whatever our station in life.

Rabindranath Tagore expressed it well when he said, 'There is no higher religion than that of sympathy for all that lives.' This sympathy – without which we dare not call ourselves truly human – is constantly born and regenerated along the haiku path.

A Muslim mystic, **Ahmad Ibn Ata'Allah**, gives out to us, and rightly so:

'Encompass with your mercy and compassion all animals and creatures. Do not say, "this is inanimate and has no awareness." Indeed, it does; it is you yourself who have no awareness!'

What are we like today? How keen is our awareness of reality? Are we much more aware than our grandparents ever were? It's debatable.

'No longer can man confront reality immediately; he cannot see it, as it were, face to face. Physical reality seems to recede in proportion as man's symbolic activity increases. Instead of dealing with the things themselves, man is in a sense constantly conversing with himself...'

— **Ernst Cassirer** (*An Essay on Man*, New Haven, Yale University Press, 1944).

40

If this be the disease, how effective is the cure:

> the pursued beetle
> just led the other into
> an empty snail shell

J. W. Hackett

Twenty years after the publication of **Cassirer's** *An Essay on Man*, the following winning entry was one of over a staggering 41,000 haiku received by the Japan Air Lines-sponsored contest in America:

> a bitter morning:
> sparrows sitting together
> without any necks

J. W. Hackett

The author, **James W. Hackett**, the first American master. Count the syllables on your fingers. This is truly a great haiku. The season and time of the day are delicately marked out for us; there is no fantasising going on, nor is there any trace of the intrusive ego. The scene is depicted, tenderly, chillingly and with compassion, which is the beginning and end of wisdom.

What would **Cassirer** have to say – well over half a century later – of our age of virtual reality. Would he not say that we are in need of the following anonymous Japanese haiku as a form of therapy?

> how refreshing—
> the whinny of a packhorse
> unburdened of everything!

Anonymous

And what would **Cassirer** have to say about the cult of personality and stardom? How refreshing that the above haiku is perfectly anonymous!

—⁓—

Innocent play ... Pornography degrades men, women and children. But when haiku touches on the erotic, the experience is usually one of innocence, surprise, awakening:

41

looking for eggs inside the barn . . .
but I've found instead
my cousin's breasts!

José Rubén Romero

Haiku and *senryu* have many moods and playfulness is one of them. **H F Noyes**, the American haikuist domiciled in Greece, elucidated this play:

'With the Mahayana Buddhist teachings that spread in the first century to China and Japan, there was a profound infusion of spiritual and cultural energy. Central to the new understanding was the Chinese character kú, a symbol of universal essence. The word haiku in Japanese may be construed to mean merely a playful verse, but as handed down to us from Bashō's day, it has had a vital spiritual element... the natural and the spiritual element cannot be separated and they form the harmonic whole we so often sense in the haiku moment. The spirit of play and the play of spirit are simultaneous and one...'

(*Ko*, 1998, Spring/Summer)

a sprinkling of light
across a murky mountainside—
goose-bearing wind

Suzuki Setsuko

mountain village—
even in my soup
the harvest moon

Issa
(David G. Lanoue)

As the 10th century collection of Japanese poems, *Kokinshú*, declares:

'Listening to the voices of the warbler that sings in the flowers or the frog that lives in the water, we ask, what of all living things does not create poetry...?'

(Quoted in *Traces of Dreams, Landscape, Cultural Memory, and the Poetry of Bashō*, Haruo Shirane, Stanford University Press, 1998)

42

field mouse
looking at its own reflection . . .
quivering whiskers

féachann luch fhéir
ar a scáil féin . . .
féasóga ar crith

writing its story
on the strand . . .
a severed branch

a scéal féin
á bhreacadh aici ar an trá
géag scoite

Sanity, health, salvation … The haikuist, like the shaman, the druid, the eco-warrior, is convinced that our relationship with Nature is essential to sanity, health and salvation. By this we do not mean that we must make a retreat in the wilderness. In the classic haiku of **Issa**, the Japanese master demonstrates extraordinary fellow-feeling for the lowliest of creatures, even the flea. Issa's heart and spirit live on:

> waiting for crumbs
> the blackbird's gold-rimmed eye
> on my freezing fingers

Ruth Robinson

—∿∿—

Before and after enlightenment … In the 9th.century an anonymous Irish monk wrote with the regaling freshness and pure awareness that we associate with haiku:

> Small bird
> from your little yellow beak
> a whistle dashed
> out over Loch Lao[1]
> blackbird
> from a branch all
> yellow-splashed

Anonymous (Ireland)

The poetic essence of a place, *hon'i* in Japanese poetics, is captured above.

Haiku – and to a certain extent the nature-poetry of the Irish, the Chinese, the Inuit and the literature of tribal peoples – roots us in a meaningful existence, reminding us of the fragile interdependence of all living things and the illusory nature of matter, as seasons turn, as vapour changes to water, to ice.

A Zen disciple described his life as hewing wood and drawing water. That was before enlightenment. After enlightenment? Hewing wood and drawing water! All very ordinary really:

---

[1] *Loch Lao / Belfast Lough*

45

late-summernight
a sheep seeks something to drink
deep in the bucket

Marcel Smets

And good fun too:

a boozer
nods
to the snowman:

Ikuyo Yoshimura

studiously, he sits,
contemplating mountains—
praiseworthy frog!

Issa

———*/W/*———

Meditative observation ... Prettification is not at the heart of haiku. Haiku
is of much sterner stuff. The haiku way of living is more than simply
observing the minutiae of natural, terrestrial phenomena in all weathers and
moods and it is much more than snapshots of flora and fauna. In meditative
observation, the haikuist peers into the life of things, 'sees eternity in a
grain of sand' and is transmuted by the encounter:

the reservoir
goes through the whole night
gargling stars

Francisco Mendez

These insights are, as it were, spontaneous gifts exchanged between humans
and creation, glimpses of cosmic consciousness, illuminating flashes when
earth and sky, heaven and the world are one and the heart is at peace:

la vasta noche
no es ahora otra cosa
            que una fragrancia

the vast night—
            now no more
                    than a fragrance

Jorge Luis Borges
(Noel Griffin)

Freshness of dust ... It was not blindness or part-blindness that heightened the Argentinean's sense of smell. There is a fragrance that accompanies the haiku experience, the haiku moment. It is the fragrance of the spheres, first cousin to the music of the spheres. It is the freshness of dust!

lodo del charco quieto:
mañana polvo
bailando en el camino

mud in a still puddle:
tomorrow's dust
dancing on the roadway

Octavio Paz
(Noel Griffin)

It is the fullness of emptiness!

up he comes
my favourite cormorant—
            empty beak!

Issa

faint sunlight
　　injecting the veins

　　　of a falling leaf

Breath of attunement ... Not everyone is capable of writing – or even reading – conventional poetry. It is a minority pursuit, in most so-called civilised nations. But the haiku is within everyone's compass. Anyone – even a child, especially a child – can write haiku, once the principle of the haiku moment is grasped. Thereafter it's a question of practising the seventeen-syllable structure in three-line configuration until it becomes second nature, and later experimenting with free-style haiku of a dozen or so syllables:

> the fleeing sandpipers
> turn about suddenly
>   and chase back the sea!

> **J. W. Hackett**

ancient pond . . .
    a frog jumps
    into the sound of water

Bashō

In one breath, **Matsuo Bashō** expresses perfect attunement. How utterly real it is! No illusion here, no doubt, no anxiety, no self-absorption, no dreaming, no showing off, no distraction, no longing, no loathing, no desire, no self-deception, no self. It is unalloyed awareness, active absorption, the pure breath of the here and now (and how that moment still rings out centuries later). Enlightenment is only a breath away… listen!

> over the dishes
>   goes the sound of rat clatter—
>   ah, how cold it is!

> **Buson**

Issa knew that haiku-poetry can be a path to enlightenment:

He believed that one part of that path is shikan, a meditative state in which perception is utterly free of discrimination between mind and matter, self and object; where the only permanence is impermanence and change, whether subtle or violent, remains the essence of being…

(The Spring of My Life)

Haiku creates a silent revolution, deepening our understanding of these truths: change is life itself and all life-cycles, governing all living organisms, including ostracised forms of life so beloved of haikuists:

slaking its thirst
with bitter ice—
a sewer rat

Bashō

Bashō spoke of *fueki ryōko*, that which is unchanging and that which is ever-changing. Haiku is born in the energies of this rich paradox.

Art of interweaving ... It is when we are cut off that enlightened perception becomes impossible. We need to learn the gentle art of interweaving and once we learn it – through haiku – it's rather like riding a bicycle, something we never forget.

Croatian haikuist and haiku theorist **Marijan Cekolj** puts it this way: 'When the interior awareness knows that the exterior awareness is waiting in a state of readiness, there is a good possibility of their interweaving in the present moment in which the Ego has never existed...' (*Smijeh Sazanja/The Laughter of Cognition*, Samobor, 1998, The Croatian Haiku Association).

——

Learning from the pine ... **Bashō's** advice, 'Learn of the pine from a pine...' is so often quoted in haiku circles as to become a shibboleth. Like all great, simple truths, it needs commentary to help us grasp the original meaning. **Isoji Asâ** comments thus:

'The way is not to divorce oneself from the pine and to see it with one's own feeling, but to divorce the self and to enter the pine with a selfless interest. Then a real insight into the pine arises. Thus will it become a pine into which the human heart has entered...It will become sentient, instead of remaining a natural object, viewed through the five senses objectively. And furthermore contemplating the human feeling infused into the object, the poet expresses it through the illumination of his insight, and when that feeling finds its expression, it becomes the art of haiku...'

(Quoted in *The Japanese Haiku* by Kenneth Yasuda, Charles E. Tuttle Company, 1957).

Embracing the 'itness' of the pine ... This is how the art critic **Bernard Berenson** (1865 – 1954) described a defining moment of consciousness: 'I climbed up a tree stump and felt suddenly immersed in Itness. I did not call it by that name. I had no need for words. It and I were one...' (*Sketch from a Self-Portrait*, Pantheon Books, 1949). Some psychologists may say that this is nothing more than our longing to return to the undifferentiated world of the womb. But it is not so. Not really. We are mammals, yes, not robots. But the haiku moment does not project us forwards or backwards, in time or space, to the security of an environment we have lost. (Though, interestingly enough, one does encounter the occasional Japanese haiku which revolves on seeing one's preserved umbilicus in later life, as an adult!) Who knows what remains of the subconscious after the haiku moment has tussled us into an awakened awareness of the here and now?

Perhaps the most meaningful arts are those which fuse the factual with the sublime, the earthly with the unearthly, the paintings of **Chagall** and **Gauguin**, the poetry of **Yeats** and **Lorca**, the *Lieder* of **Schubert**, the short stories of **Isaac Bashevis Singer**, haiku such as this:

> wild geese, wild geese
> sleeting through
> the ebbing stars

> **Seán Mac Mathúna**

Life of connection ... We propose, therefore, in this book, that the haiku way of living is one of connectedness. For too long the intellectual fashion was to be the outsider, the wry observer of a world of mayhem, cruelty and meaninglessness. Haiku challenges this dehumanising legacy of disenchantment. Writing in *A Heart as Wide as the World: Living with Mindfulness, Wisdom, Compassion* (Shambhala, 1997) **Sharon Salzberg** claims that 'a life of connection and authenticity can come completely alive in us now.' This claim we make for haiku today, without fear of contradiction. Test its validity for yourself. The haiku moment is real. It is not a *fata morgana*. It is not a vision in the clouds. The haiku path is a path through this world, a path of tolerance, compassion and fearless engagement, not one of complacency.

Issa, the tenderest of poets and author of more than 20,000 haiku, could be critical of society when he saw fit:

people? forget it!
even the scarecrows,
crooked to a man!

Issa

And, elsewhere, he complains:

only some of the nightingales
visiting my scraggy hedge
know how to sing

Issa

Is he really complaining though? Remember his favourite cormorant earlier on, the one that caught nothing!

What is it about a feckless cormorant, a less than perfect nightingale, an orphaned sparrow that warms the heart of **Issa**?

It is something beautifully anti-heroic that has been called *hogan-biiki*, a sympathy for the outcast, the defeated, the underdog. It is one of the greatest gifts of haiku to poetry and to mankind.

—◦◦◦—

Healing balsam … The healing balsam of haiku, ancient and new, is needed now more than ever in our age of rapidly decreasing bio-diversity, irredeemable cultural and linguistic impoverishment and the ravaging of natural resources.

hey, leave him alone!
the fly rubs his hands,
rubs his legs

Issa

R. H. Blyth says the haiku path is non-emotional. This may or may not be true. **Issa**, above, shows love for the fly, does he not? Indeed **Yoshiko Yoshino** is bold enough to state: 'When making haiku, mere observation, however detailed and precise, is just not enough. Once love is sent towards the object, the object responds…' (Quoted in *Tsuru*, Yoshiko Yoshino, Trans. Lee Gurga & Emiko Miyashita, Deep North Press, 2001)

Is reality – so-called – what makes the news? The following anonymous haiku is not the makings of newspaper headline. There is very little happening. But is it less real for that?

> nothing
> seems to be going on:
> insects chirping

Anonymous

Is this too insignificant to record? Nothing is insignificant on the haiku path! Consider this: 'That which fleets by has great significance. The most delicate things are the ones that in the end prove strongest.' (**Seamus Heaney**, *Chicago Tribune*, June 3, 2001)

> just a minnow
> the granite mountain wobbles
> on the lake

Christopher Herold

—*∿∿*—

Invitation to play ...Think of what might happen if children all over the world had the opportunity to enjoy and explore the spirit of haiku for half an hour each week, in sessions devoted to reading, composition, quiet reflection and discussion. Might we create a better world, a less violent world, a world more loved than it is now?

> january storm
> the bamboo loves
> to thrash about

Robert Gibson
(*Children of the Sparrow: HAIKU*, Seattle, 1999)

Do we exclude the spirit of haiku from the curriculum in our efforts to 'create' 'successful', efficient people who will 'grasp' whatever opportunities they can in later life and 'control' the world they live in?

53

in the silence
after snow
a wren's faint chirp

Rich Krivcher
(*Fallen Leaves*, Ed. **John Leonard**, San Francisco, 2000)

Issa tells us in *Oraga haru* (The Spring of my Life) that he was only six years old when he wrote:

my wee sparrows,
you too are without a mother—
come play with me!

Issa

—⁓⁓—

Merging, the ultimate sacrament ... To be slightly technical for a moment, the touching haiku above contains *ada*, the freshness of child-like vision. It also contains what you will find in some of the best haiku, what the Japanese call *butsuga ichinyo*, the identification of the poet with his subject. In much of conventional literature, we praise the author's 'distance', as the French have it. In haiku, self merges with object. In this very merging is the sacrament, the dynamics of enlightenment.

Haiku is a complete, universal, effortless path in itself. At the core of the flurry, flux and excitement of life is ineffable stillness and imperturbability, the 'Be still and know I am thy God' attested to by mystics of all creeds and none.

The haikuist comes to the haiku moment unburdened by prejudice and doctrine. 'If thine eye causeth thee to sin, pluck it out!' Such masochistic advice is foreign to the nature of the haikuist's vision. Closer would be the advice from the *Candamaharoshana-tantra*:

When you see form, look!
            Similarly, listen to sounds,
            Inhale scents,
            Taste delicious flavours,
            And feel textures . . .

The New Testament tells us, 'Unless ye be like children, ye cannot enter the Kingdom of Heaven.' The haiku moment restores our child-like innocence and is ready to happen whenever our lives appear 'stale and unprofitable.' **Supplying the words ...** Ultimately, the haiku path is not a didactic one. Life itself offers us an eternal, textless sermon for which we merely supply the words and that which reverberates behind the word:

> autumn wind:
> gods, Buddha—
> lies, lies, lies
>
> ### Shiki

Haiku can be a daily, weekly or monthly spring-cleaning of the mind and spirit, leaving us with such an openness of heart that our sense of being alive is almost staggering:

> if it rains
> from the distant sky, let it rain!
> if the wind blows, let it blow!
>
> ### Ryokan

Lightness of being ... Let us demystify enlightenment! What is *satori* (in Zen), *samadhi* (in Hinduism) but the dissolving of the ego. Similarly, the Tantric concept of *maithuna* relates to that falling away of the ego in sacramental, sexual union. The haiku moment is a powerfully charged, focussed glimpse of unity and non-differentiation, its sheer pleasure reminding us of our birthright, its passing an eloquent portent of impermanence and mutability.

For most of us, the divine transports and ecstasies of **St. Teresa of Avila**, of **Rumi**, or of **Mirabai** are closed doors. Our lifestyle, our habits, our diet ... maybe even our neighbours ... everything seems to conspire to close the gates of such exalted realms to us. **Ramakrishna** described an instant:

'It was as if houses, doors, temples, and everything else vanished altogether; as if there was nothing anywhere. And what I saw was an infinite shoreless sea of light, a sea that was consciousness...'

In haiku, we take our enlightenment in smaller, more manageable doses as we experience the dissolving of ego, its coming and going:

> in the river reflection
> he watches himself
> watch the sunset

Alan J. Summers
(in *paper wasp*, Australia, 1997)

There is a relaxed feeling of lightness – *karumi* – in the above haiku, employing everyday syntax and easily recognised imagery. *Karumi* became **Bashō's** ideal in the final phase of his development.

—⁓—

Fabric of consciousness ... Haiku can accompany all of us along the path of life, not as a diary or archive of what we have seen, experienced or felt but, rather, as a living testimony to a developed, ever-evolving, instinctual awareness of having actually lived a life impregnated by reality – whatever our circumstances. This awareness colours and strengthens the fabric of our consciousness, into and out of the sunset of our lives:

> growing older—
> more of this haiku,
> more turnip soup

Kyoshi

> at last, death!
> little by little
> the odour of potions vanishing

Dakotsu

The African-American writer **Richard Wright** wrote thousands of haiku during his self-exile in France. His daughter Julia remarks: 'I believe his haiku were self-developed antidotes against illness, and that breaking down words into syllables matched the shortness of his breath...' (*Haiku, This Other World* by Richard Wright, Arcade Publishing, New York, 1998).

—⁓—

Become a *haijin*! Practising haiku leads us, inexorably, to an awareness of our awareness. **D. T. Suzuki** (profiled in the *New Yorker*, August 31, 1957) remarked: 'The intuitive recognition of the instant, and thus reality, is regarded by Zen practitioners as the highest act of wisdom…'

Don't overlook the word 'act'. The path of haiku, while effortless, is not for the lily-livered. It is a profound engagement with life itself. *Haii*, the spirit of haiku, is boundless, eternal.

—∿∿—

Takahama Kyoshi (1874 –1959) composed thousands of haiku in the course of a long life:

a woman washes herself
    in a tub—
        a crow stares

Takahama Kyoshi

Not something one sees every day, an ogling crow, and yet what a haunting image it is.

Fukio (1903 –1930) had a much shorter life but also wrote riveting haiku:

the heart of winter—
a crow perches
on its own shadow

Fukio

This has the quality of *sabi* or loneliness. It is the opposite of the flowery, the showy. Haiku does not close its eyes to drabness, bareness, raggedness, homelessness.

What a shame it would be to live a life, short or long, happy or sad, without knowing one has witnessed unique, haunting moments.

The haikuist is alive to the world and open to a host of impressions that may never quite penetrate those of duller or jaded senses. What are our senses for but to make our way in this world as fulfilled, enlightened human beings?

I'm leaving—
have as much sex as you like,
my flies

Issa

Confrontation ... To this day, hundreds of thousands of Japanese enjoy
composing haiku, and travel in bus-loads to view cherry blossoms, plum
blossoms... a harmless activity, one might say. But it would be a mistake to
see the haiku path as one of charming innocence, respite, or mere escapism
in a world still ravaged by war, starvation, poverty, disease and suppression.

Haiku does not shirk conflict, as was illustrated in a remarkable,
confrontational collection of war haiku published in Croatia in 1995:

a fallen soldier.
how loud the ticking
of the watch

Enes Kiševic

a body falls
dissolving the snow
into a red ice

Ivica Jembrih

We are not spared the horrors of war in this unflinching testimony since it is
the haikuist's vocation to look at, not look away:

in the burned-out village
a wounded stray dog
sniffing charred bones

Vladimir Devidé

Amid the bombings, from out of the smoke, the screams, among severed
limbs, nature emerges, somewhat incongruously. Life? A glimmer of hope?
Out of all this gore and destruction? Meaning? In the midst of
meaninglessness?

58

a red poppy
between the rails
stops the trains

Smiljka Bilankov

with its big cobweb
a spider mended
the demolished roof

Luko Paljetak

These haiku restore some sense, even some dignity, to an apocalyptic situation; they display the versatility of haiku in handling the most extreme vicissitudes of life. A sane, resilient response to insanity. Silence in the face of exploding shells. Enlightenment dawning through the ghostly smoke rising from the rubble.

During the Sino-Japanese war, many haiku were found on the dead bodies of soldiers:

foreign soil—
violets, your colour
your fragrance hasn't changed!

Anonymous

There's a saying in Irish, *beatha an tsaighdiúra, beatha na muice* – 'the life of a soldier, the life of a pig'. Both are fed for the slaughter! Haiku consciousness emphasises the fragility of life, the futility of war:

lilacs by the bridge—
soldier after soldier
catching the scent

Ernest Sherman
(*Modern Haiku*, 31.3, Fall 2000)

Boredom, cynicism, ennui and other negative states of mind can be avoided by taking the visionary path of haiku:

a tide-cluttered beach;
  this clear chunk of jellyfish
  magnifies the sand

R. Christopher Thorsen

—/w—

Haiku and health ... Might haiku be actually good for our health? If the haiku moment is a form of meditation, then why not? People in the healing professions should try to use haiku as a therapeutic tool.

Human relations ... Relationships, too, become deepened, heightened, by experiencing and expressing them in haiku and *senryu*:

  the scent of the forest
   on their shoes,
  father and son asleep on the train

Ikuyo Yoshimura

 a cold shiver—
 stepping on my dead wife's
 comb

Buson

The haikuist's relationships extend to all the living and the dead, embracing and being embraced at the same moment:

   a winter's day,
   a frozen shadow
   on my nag

Bashō

Haiku enlightenment – living the life of haiku – changes the way we behave, subtly refining our actions:

> leaving a patch
> unmowed,
> wild strawberries

Elizabeth Searle Lamb

Flawed creatures that we are, abstract notions of virtue and ideals of *ahimsa* (non-violence) – the usual moral precepts, or commandments – do not always transfer to daily life. Living according to the spirit of haiku is to be aware. In this awareness, our higher nature is allowed to express itself naturally, in word and deed:

> come on then, beetle,
> walking over my foot—
>   you go first!

David Cobb

The ripple effect of such words and deeds is immeasurable and crisscrosses the world. As **Kenneth Yasuda** observed (and as we will have gathered already):

'A haiku moment is a kind of aesthetic moment – a moment in which the words which created the experience and the experience itself can become one. The nature of a haiku moment is anti-temporal and its quality is eternal, for in this state man and his environment are one unified whole, in which there is no sense of time...'

— **Kenneth Yasuda** (*The Japanese Haiku*, Charles E. Tuttle Company, 1957).

Preparing for the haiku moment – or not ... You may ask, how does one prepare for the haiku moment? Conscious preparation may lead us nowhere. An ancient Zen scripture admonishes us as follows: 'Don't dwell on anything, yet enliven the mind.' (Quoted in *Zen Antics*, translated and edited by **Thomas Cleary**, Shambhala, 1993). It is best not to prepare for the haiku moment, while keeping the above precept on the back-burner. The outrageousness of Zen – grabbing you by the scruff of the neck and putting you standing on your head – is one way towards gaining an insight into the spontaneity of haiku enlightenment; but it could also be a dead end. If it doesn't work for you, drop it – and be quick about it!

Having said that, many would argue that Zen has proved to have universal application. 'Among the diverse roots of Japanese civilisation,' claims **Thomas Cleary**, 'Buddhism is pre-eminent in providing an intellectual outlook that can transcend national cultures and sustain a genuine egalitarian global vision...'(*Rational Zen*, Shambhala, 1992).

Zen Buddhism may or may not be a suitable introduction towards preparing for the experience of haiku enlightenment. Here is another way to look at the problem. It comes from Dutch author **Cees Nooteboom** in a book about Spain, *Roads to Santiago* (The Harvill Press, 1997):

> '*Sternstunde*, a wonderful word in German, defining a particular moment in life, a "starry hour" that has been or will be so important that it will change life's course. The notion presupposes a stroke of enlightenment, a sublime flash of insight, a shock of recognition, and I am much too intractable a character to believe in that kind of thing. Surely whatever it is that has suddenly required illumination must have been there already, in a state of latency. How else could you recognise the moment?'

A Zen master or a haiku practitioner might not disagree.

—*∿*—

Side-stepping regret and remorse ... Too many lives are steeped in regret and remorse. Too many of us know the meaning of **Tennyson's** 'tears from the depth of some divine despair'. Haiku can step in before regret is possible, confronting reality so that the shocks and upheavals of life do not unbalance us. By facing the exigencies of daily life in the spirit of haiku, how can things catch up on us unawares?

my ailing father
listening to the crickets
last day of August

F M Black

As we have pointed out previously, death itself need not catch us unawares. *Jisei*, death poems, could be said to be a genre all of its own. Here from *Blithe Spirit*, June 1988, is **Norman Barraclough's** 'death poem':

on the moor
wind-chased ripples run
into still water

Norman Barraclough

Albrecht Dürer said a long time ago: 'For verily, art is embedded in Nature; he who can extract it, has it…'

the other shore
is calling us . . .
as is the shore we left

彼の岸が
我ら呼ぶ
此の岸のごと

(Mariko Sumikura)

an caladh thall
ag glaoch orainn . . .
is an caladh a d'fhágamar

Channelling natural wisdom ... Whatever about this century, the 20th century will not be described as an Age of Faith. Uncertainty seems to be the order of the day and conspiracy theories have cult-like popularity. Those who tenaciously cling to doctrinal tenets are deemed fundamentalists, extremists, 'unlettered' peasants, Flat Earthists, Luddites and the like. Society seems to need scapegoats.

Such are the complexities of modern life that artists search for a voice to convincingly handle a variation on the theme of 'we do not know' and quite a few resort to shock tactics. Haiku stands out in this world by confidently proclaiming that there is quite a lot we know, a lot we can intuit, much we can learn, by channelling our own natural wisdom:

> they come to the marsh
> cooling their hooves —
> autumn deer

Keiko Akamatsu

Because of its compactness, haiku says just what it wants to say while containing more than it appears to say. Elaboration would be gilding the lily, smothering the stark truth of the haiku moment:

> stillborn—
> only the mother's cry
> echoes down the hall

Peter Duppenthaler

Enlightenment on the haiku path is not synonymous with bubbling happiness. It can be chilling. But where there's life there's a promise of warmth:

> young bucks
> licking each other . . .
> morning frost

Issa
(David G. Lanoue)

> warm rain before dawn
> my milk flows into her
> unseen

Ruth Yarrow

PAUSE

We are about half-way through this section.
Definitely time for another pause.

Take a breather.

Slow down.

Do something else.

Do something you've never done before…

Say something you always intended to say, but never got around to.

Or be *stumm*, silent.

Accept who you are and the gift of silence which comes with this…

Enlightenment and you ... The word 'enlightenment' in our title has attracted you, has it not? Otherwise this book would not be in your hands.

We hope you did pause above. You see, the body-mind is a delicate mechanism. Let's not overdose. You needn't close your eyes. Stay awake and reflect on this for a minute. You were not attracted by the word 'enlightenment'. Enlightenment was attracted to you. Savour this enigma. Then we can continue, together. But savour it well! Indeed, the best way to read this book is to pause after each haiku. Yes, after each one. Allow time for full absorption. And for transformation.

———w———

Seeing is believing ... A theme running through this book is the importance of seeing. Some of us need to be taught how to see. **Heinrich Böll** recalled in *What's to Become of the Boy?* (Northwestern University Press, 1996):

'For a time I must have been walking with my head down, since one day my father offered me a prize if I could name twenty-five stores between St. Severin's Church and Perlen-Graben. I lifted my head once again and won the prize...'

Of course, even with heads down we can see. We can see from wherever we are now, even from habitual angles:

'In a certain town there lived a cobbler, Martin Avdéich by name. He had a tiny room in a basement, one window of which looked out on the street. Through it he could see only the feet of those who passed by, but Martin recognised many people by their boots, which he had repaired...'

— **Leo Tolstoy** (*Twenty Three Tales*, Oxford University Press).

What may be an exotic image to one person can be quite everyday to another, as in these two examples from *Haiku Moment*:

the dugs of the old cow
shrivelled—
late autumn wind

Joe Nutt

spot of sunlight—
on a blade of grass the dragonfly
changes its grip

Lee Gurga

The nature of the image is not important; what matters is the moment of perception. Perception is more than seeing. *Chambers Twentieth Century Dictionary* defines 'perception' as: 'act or power of perceiving: discernment: apprehension of any modification of consciousness: the combining of sensations into a recognition of an object...'

In *Webster's Third New International Dictionary* one of the uses of 'perceive' is given in an illustrative sentence by **Norbert Muehlen**:... 'people have become so used to the sights of ruins that they hardly perceive them anymore.'

Precisely! Perceived by the haikuist, the ordinary becomes extraordinary. As **Jim Kacian** reminds us:... 'If haiku affords us moments of vision, it is not so much that we are visionaries, as that up to that moment we have been blind...' (*Frogpond*, 1998, Vol. XXI, No. 2, Haiku Society of America).

Haiku and the city ... Can one write haiku in towns and cities? Of course! Rain falls on cities too. And snow. The sun shines, or does not shine. Cities have gardens and parks. There's always the zoo ... why not visit your nearest zoo and compose zoo-ku!

Some cities have urban foxes, urban monkeys and, for all one knows, alligators in the sewers. Cities have men, women and children, insects, markets, flower stalls, aromas and textures:

moonlight
reducing the city
to ruins

Seán Mac Mathúna

Nature's ability to manifest itself amid the hubbub of urban life can add poignancy to haiku as in the following American and Japanese vignettes:

the city bus stops—
a caw of a winter crow
through the opened door

Robert Spiess

—◦◦◦—

Unique and alone ... Each one of us is unique and we are alone. We may
enjoy the love of family, the conviviality of friends and the esteem of
colleagues, but – whether we do or not – ultimately we are alone. For all
that, we are intimately linked to everything in the universe, animate and
inanimate, and to each other. (**Hermes** says no tear is shed in a vacuum).
Our relationships change, inevitably, since change is the nature of growth.
Haiku moments vividly capture the vulnerability of our shared existence:

orphaned duckling
sticking close
to the water lily

David Mills

This is something the haikuist once saw and may never see again. 'If an
event is unrepeatable, that is beauty…' says **Soen Nakagawa** in *Endless
Vow* (Shambhala, 1996).

Easter evening—
the old woman gathers
her unsold flowers

Ion Codrescu

(The use of a seasonal topic is known as *kidai*. *Kigo* is the actual word, or
phrase, that conveys *kidai*. We can have our own seasonal, cultural or
religious festivals to replace the traditional 5 seasons in the Japanese haiku
tradition – spring, summer, autumn, winter, New Year).

In dreams, in meditation, in prayer, in revelry, it often seems that we
are not utterly alone, that no one is ever totally alone, that the myriad dead
live on, that the whole universe is teeming with ghosts, humans, gods,
demi-gods, angels, demons, imps, fairies… Our dreams, our myths, our
songs, our legends, these too are part of a greater pattern of reality:

in my dream my father
talks about summer projects
not knowing he's dead

Alain Kervern

(This has the quality of *makoto*, honesty, sincerity, unaffectedness).

———

Relics and rubbish ... The more haiku you read and write, the more you are likely to discard. One in ten will satisfy you at first. Later, maybe only one in a hundred. This is as it should be.

The very notion of haiku enlightenment itself should be consigned to the rubbish heap, for a period, lest it become an obsession! **Krishnamurti** (**J.** that is, not **U. G.**) says in *Thoughts on Living*, 'Truth is a pathless land. There is no guide, no law, no tradition which will lead you to it but your own constant and intelligent awareness.'

father presses olives,
we dip our bread
in the first oil

Marinko Kovacevic
(*Committed to the Road,* The Association of Croatia Haiku Poets)

Constant and intelligent awareness. This is the gift of haiku. What you do with that gift is your own business but why not use it to live an enlightened life?

On the haiku path (or pathlessness), blink and you miss it! **Bruce Ross**, editor of *Haiku Moment, An Anthology of Contemporary North American Haiku* (Tuttle, 1993) offers the apprentice some hope, however:

'Underlying this emphasis on the given moment of time is the Buddhist idea that the world is made anew each moment. A kind of divine spontaneity thus inheres in each moment...'

In the West, we are rapidly losing a sense of the sacred, of the *temenos*, the holy place. We regard with some amusement the Japanese belief that after 99 years, cooking utensils take on the significance of holy relics.

———

Constant regeneration … Defining ultimate reality is not the business of haiku. What is ultimate reality? A mathematical formula? Our realities are coloured by our moods, our temperament, our language, our culture, our beliefs and so on – throw in the weather, the contents of our stomach, our ailments, and the list becomes surreal.

The haikuist can only claim to capture a moment of reality – and a succession of such moments. These moments are intuited and caught in all their transience and uniqueness and are streamlined with the constant regeneration of the world:

> she brings a snowflake inside
> saying
> look how big it is

Sean Burn

Haiku is simply seeing. Seeing, simply:

> yellow dandelion
> head above
> the young nettles

Zoran Dederović

Aloneness predicates the possibility of oneness:

> evening feeding—
> old farmer's breath
> smokes out to his cows

Randy M. Brooks

—∿∿—

Instinct … In his *Record of the Little Garden*, **Masaoka Shiki** wrote:

'Just then a yellow butterfly came flying by and as I watched it forage among the flowers in the hedge, my soul began to move out to it as though by instinct…'

(*Masaoka Shiki* by Janine Beichman, Kodansha International, 1986)

All art forms have therapeutic uses. Haiku is particularly effective in coming to terms with loss, with grief, submerged memories, old wounds. **Chiyo-ni** grieves for her lost son:

> dragon-fly hunter:
> where has he wandered off to?
> where?

Chiyo-ni

Allow old desires, old sorrows, disappointments, pangs, attachments to flow into the light of the now in a mature spirit of acceptance:

> autumn wind—
> in the attic
> love letters yellowing

Sylvia Forges-Ryan

If you placed a book such as this in the library of the nearest prison, hospital, nursing home or school, might it change lives? It might – it might even change the way we view our pets, not to mention our neighbours:

> our dog licks
> my reflection
> in the cold puddle

Scott Hall

—〜〜—

Way of the gentle warrior ... If the traditional martial arts of the East are said to bring us to a state of balance, poise, flexibility and readiness, a state in which we anticipate a blow to the body, or, indeed, deliver a blow, the way of haiku could be described as the way of the gentle warrior:

> by a raindrop
> struck, snail
> closes up

Buson

How immediate this is! The author lived between 1716-1783 – but this haiku is ever-new.

Rain is common enough in world poetry – where rain occurs. In the poetry of India, a dark rain-cloud can represent a divinity, a harbinger of fruitfulness. But how often does one find a single raindrop in a poem? In **Buson's** haiku it strikes a snail! One is reminded of the cold accuracy of martial arts! And yes, haiku must make a direct hit if it is to be hair-raisingly effective.

The word *zenkan* could be applied to many haiku in this book. The word means, simply, pure seeing, momentary, instant enlightenment:

> in a pool of stars
> a frog is hopping
> from one to the other

> **Robert Bebek**

This is a charming example of the effectiveness of **Dōgen's** dictum in action – 'forgetting oneself is being enlightened by all things'. We cannot forget ourselves by a mere act of will and determination. We can go into a stupor with the aid of narcotics or induce a comatose state by hammering our heads with a mallet… Forgetting ourselves while still remaining conscious – more conscious than ever – this is what we sow and reap simultaneously in the field of haiku enlightenment.

Haiku does not seek to obliterate our consciousness of who we are. Au contraire, it sharpens our sense of who and what we really are, as **Seishi** observed, dramatically:

> every cry
> of the butcher-bird
> says what I am

> **Seishi**

Contemplate the following by **Issa**:

> falling from my heart
> the snows
> of Shinano

> **Issa**

This is an outstanding example of Advaita, non-duality. The border, the barrier, between the inner and the outer world is down. All is realized in the heart, in the shining Self. The interior and the exterior worlds are momentarily one. What a blessed moment he has described. Take this haiku, this jewel, to your heart.

T
H
I
N
K

Seeing truly is not merely a change in the direction of seeing, but a change at its very centre, in which the seer himself disappears.

— **Ramesh S. Balsekar**

A
B
O
U
T

I
T

Jim Norton, an Irish *haijin*, writing in *redthread, Newsletter of the Haiku Sangha* (February 2002) admonishes us to hear with the whole body! This is what **Seishi** was doing in his butcher-bird haiku. It is what **Ikkyu** was doing, in his boat on Lake Biwa, when – caaaaw! – a crow furnished him with *satori*.

> cricket chirp—
> how clear
> my life is now

> **Hakuu**

Norton gives us an apt quote, reminding us how essential to the haiku path is the aural dimension:

> 'If our listening is partial, there is still an I who is listening, and our listening is tainted by this. Simply listen. It is only when listening is complete that the enlightened mind appears. But we are always listening. We are listening now. We listen with our ears; with our eyes; with our nose ... we listen with every cell and pore of our body...'

> (*Going Beyond Buddha: The Awakening Practice of Listening*, Dae Gak, Tuttle, 1997)

This is an electrifying insight. Walking the haiku path can create goose-pimples – and, listen, they are listening!

> first to meet my ear—
> the stream that flows
> by my native village

> **Hosha**

—⁓—

Wake up ... We can take a communal, compositional stroll, or *ginko*, creating and then comparing haiku with like-minded friends; or, in this age of increased mobility, we can take our haiku notebooks with us on our travels:

4 a.m.
> first the cockerel
> now the donkey

John Barlow
(*Flamingo Shapes*, Snapshot Press 2001)

—*ᴧᴧᴧ*—

Promise of haiku … R. H. Blyth, whose 4-volume *Haiku* (Hokuseido Press, 1949) is essential reading for all who wish to follow this path, believed that writing (and reading) haiku is a spiritual exercise in which we instantly blossom into a state of mind, 'in which we are not separated from other things, are indeed identical with them, and yet retain our own individuality…' This is true. This is the sacred promise of haiku.

The non-appearance of the personal pronoun throughout this book, and in most of the haiku examples given, does not imply any diminution of the individuality or personality.

—*ᴧᴧᴧ*—

Sympathetic vibrations … A haiku may zoom in on one particular object of clear-eyed scrutiny:

> take care grasshopper—
> you become one with the leaf
> only when you're still

Robert Bebek

This is known as *ichibutsu shitate*. A haiku may also combine two distinct images, or happenings, which exchange a sympathetic timbre:

> fish-vendor testing
> the knife's edge—
> cry of seagulls

GR

This type of resonance or combination is known as *toriawase*. The dash with which the second line ends is the Western equivalent of the *kireji* or cutting word.

77

So much can be encapsulated in this smallest of literary forms. The wren's nest is a perfect fit. It is sufficient to the wren, as the Irish proverb has it (*Is leor don dreoilín a nead*). A hazel nut is the size it should be. Why should it be as big as a turnip? The genetic engineer who comes up with a turnip the size of a hazelnut should go and get his head examined. To quote (or misquote) **William of Occam**: 'It is a sin to do with more what can be done with less!' The cultivation of haiku can deepen our day-to-day understanding of the mountains of needless waste in the world.

A ten-line haiku would not be a haiku. It would be unable to hold the energies of a haiku, it would become diffuse, a reflective, discursive or descriptive poem. **Roland Barthes**, the insightful French critic, writes: 'Haiku brevity is not formal; haiku is not a complex thought reduced to a short form but a short event which finds its right form in a touch.' (*L'empiere des signes*, Flammarion, Paris, 1970).

Simply mastering the haiku form will not bring sudden enlightenment. It is the spirit of haiku which matters and this has been eloquently attested to by **Humberto Senegal**, President of the Colombian Haiku Society:

'Erudition and intellectual wisdom, the paths of the egotistic poet, are not adequate for one who seriously wishes to draw near to haiku...'

And he goes on to warn potential haikuists:

'In the West, few cultivators of the haiku go beyond form. They focus on this part of the legacy from the masters because it seems easier to count syllables or to tie themselves to the seasons than to present themselves, and their wonder, to that same astonishment which Bashō must have experienced at the trees in bloom, at the sound of the birds and at the sound of the rain...'

The word 'astonishment' is apt and **Goethe** suggests it as a vehicle towards 'the highest summit to which the human spirit can ascend':

> linking heaven
> and this world,
> a spider's filament

Hoshino Tsubaki
(Version by ST in *World Haiku Review*, March 2003)

But let's return to **Senegal's** insights. Without them, we are not truly on the haiku path:

'Spirit is not discovering through intelligence, manipulation of literary data, academic disciplines, memorisations of literary techniques, nor through the study of complicated books and the analysis of theory and content. Spirit is only discovered through the grace of wonder and amazement...'

Unless you recognise the truth of **Senegal's** pronouncements and adhere to this simple truth, through thick and thin, the promise behind this book – sudden enlightenment through haiku – will not be fulfilled for you. From the same source, two more pronouncements then, for extra measure:

'Every haiku, when authentic, is *satori*, an ecstasy of the observed and the observer in union and manifestation, thanks to the simplicity and impersonality of the poet...'

Finally, **Senegal** emphasises another thread running through this book, namely the universality of haiku:

'To understand Bashō, his poetry, his work and his literary aesthetics is to uncover the here and now, the spirit of being, within ourselves and the world around us. And this spirit which exists in millions of forms does not belong to any culture, man, literary school, philosophy or any one religion...'

(*Round the Pond*, ed. Ion Codrescu, Editura Muntenia, Constanta, Romania, 1994).

—⁓—

Severed link ... A Breton scholar of Japanese studies, **Alain Kervern**, writing in the same Romanian publication, suggests that nomadism may still form part of our consciousness, a nomadism replaced 'by the Neolithic revolution, with fixed settlements, thanks to cattle breeding and lands to plough. Considering the long presence of men on earth, which can be estimated at hundreds of thousands of years, the Neolithic period is a recent one, and the sedentary way of life is a very new phenomenon, by comparison...'

The haiku way of life reconnects us, therefore, to Nature and will do so even when we live, or holiday, in outer space. **Bashō** referred to Nature as *zôka*, meaning creation and transformation. **Deena Metzger** (*Intimate Nature: The Bond Between Women and Animals*, Fawcett Columbine, 1998) sees the modern reaction to **Darwin** as 'a terrified lunge away from the reality of our animal natures' while **Seyyed Hossein** (*Religion and the Order of Nature*, Oxford University Press, 1996) calls for 'a resacralisation of nature'.

In effect, what many insightful ecologists and philosophers are telling us today is that we should feel we belong to this earth, that the colonial phase of extending mankind's influence to far-flung corners of the earth – and into outer space – must be replaced by a new concept, namely the colonist becoming native.

Haikuists already feel that they are 'natives' of this earth and never before has our planet been in need of such caring wisdom.

The way of haiku is a way of relating to species older than ourselves, even to often abhorred species such as the rat, said to be as numerous as ourselves:

> July afternoon—
> a couple of river rats
> grooming their whiskers
>
> **C M Buckaway**
> (*Haiku Moment*)

In some haiku, the vision seems to penetrate beyond the normal reach of vision, into the secret heart of Nature herself. This, by **Bashō**:

> night, silently
> a worm in moonlight
> boring into a chestnut
>
> **Bashō**

While classical Japanese haiku often show a subtle blend of religious influences – Buddhism, Zen Buddhism, Daoism, Shinto as well as various literary influences, Chinese mostly, Nature herself often wins out against formal codes and beliefs:

> not yet, please!
> don't ring the temple bell,
> blossoms might fall
>
> **Shigeyori**

Consciousness of evanescence opens the doors of wisdom:

our life is thinner
than a piece of paper:
snow in springtime

Shiki Matsudaira
(*Let us Write Haiku* by Sakuzô Takada
Toranomon Haiku Group, no date)

—◠◠◠—

T
H
I
N
K

The less you have the more
you are – it is accumulation
that robs you of being.

— **Karl Marx**

A
B
O
U
T

I
T

Plum flowers ... As we grow older, life seems to offer fewer surprises for us. We've seen it all and the latest headlines only confirm our suspicions. On the haiku path, however, we remain surprised. The universe is never drained of mystery. Perhaps this is its greatest gift:

> plucking the scent
> of white flowers at night, then
> plum flowers!

> **Yayu Yokoi**

The haiku path offers this eternal renewal of the spirit, It is constant, effortless work. In 1693, then aged fifty, **Bashō** declared, 'I write to discipline myself...'

All that glistens ... Those who seek enlightenment are often duped by the word 'enlightenment' itself, as if the word promises brilliance, a world and a mind awash in pure light. It can be so, but not necessarily so. In *Instant Zen, Waking Up in the Present* (North Atlantic Books, 1994), **Thomas Cleary** has translated general lectures on Zen by **Foyan** (1067 –1120) in which **Foyan's** master tells him:

> 'Learning Zen is called a gold and dung phenomenon. Before you understand it, it's like gold; when understood, it's like dung.'

If you intuit the wisdom of this, you already know what haiku enlightenment is all about.

> such grace!
> the abbot squats again today—
> bleak wintry fields

> **Buson**

Of course, more than dung is on offer. The haiku path promises this much to the dedicated haiku initiate: freedom-through-engagement – freedom from the myriad distractions that assault us from every side, from without and from within, the flowering of a dynamic, ethical consciousness and a return to the roots of our innate Buddha-nature.

Haiku is a perfect vehicle for this on-going process, bypassing cognition and intellectualisation, intuitively sublimating the duality of our existence, momentarily finding ourselves nowhere, everywhere, here on the boundless path:

> 'Just like the empty sky that does not increase or decrease – so with our mind – what need could there be to augment or amend it?'

> > — **Layman P'ang** (*A Man of Zen, The Recorded Sayings of Layman P'ang*, translated by Ruth Fuller Sasaki, Yoshitake Iriya & Dana Fraser, Weatherhill/Inklings, 1992)

> > > settling, white dew
> > > does not choose—
> > > each drop finds its home

> > > > **Soin**

—~~~—

Glimpse of timelessness … We are in time – in haiku time – and in time-stopping time – and haiku time gives us an insight into the mysterious fluidity of time:

> *speal mo sheanathar*
> > *ag meirgiú sa scioból—*
> > > *clapsholas fómhair*

> > my grandfather's scythe
> > > rusting in the barn—
> > > > autumn twilight

> > > **Cathal Ó Searcaigh**

This is a perfect example of the quality of oldness and loneliness that is called *sabi* (from the verb *sabiru*, 'to rust'!)

Haiku can give us, too, a glimpse of timelessness:

> *En el espacio*
> *esa forma sin tiempo:*
> *la luna nueva*

> > > that timeless form:
> > > the new moon
> > > in space

> > **Jorge Luis Borges**
(quoted in *Haiku International Anthology*, Ed. Zoe Savina, Athens, 2000)

im frühlingssturm
tanzen
alte blätter vom herbst

> in the spring storm
> old autumn leaves
> are dancing

> **Georg Gisi**
> (*ibid.*)

Haiku time is time now, time past, time future, time continuous:

> the sunset glow—
> Hiroshima
> as if still burning

> **Yasuhiko Shigemoto**
> (*ibid.*)

Time suspended:

> with his golden eyes
> glittering, a sleeping snake
> in hibernation

> **Makoto Tamaki**
> (*ibid.*)

It is time and space, recreating themselves in the cosmic dance, always taking on old-new forms, new-old shapes, old-new sounds:

> a hum
> from the north
> grows into swans above me

> **Tsunehiko Hoshino**
> (*ibid.*)

Diligence and awareness come with haiku and are necessary virtues along the true haiku path if we are to avoid the delusions of false enlightenment. After all, in his lofty Bavarian retreat, Hitler would stare at the mountains and when the moon appeared he used to say that his mind would fill with brightness… Clearly, therefore, a balmy suffusion of light is hardly sufficient to transform our hearts and minds. Thankfully, the discipline of haiku is on the side of life and inner light:

> pregnant again…
> the fluttering of moths
> against the window
>
> **Janice M. Bostok**
> (*ibid.*)

Haiku is the promise of new life, hope and regeneration, albeit in a world of impermanence:

> frost on the grass:
> fickle form
> there and not there
>
> **Zaishiki**

—◠◠◠—

Let's pause again … Yes, do take another break now, lest verbiage get in our way. You could go to a mirror, for instance, and have a good laugh at yourself. Seriously! Or flick back and read again that luminous haiku by **Issa** on the snows of Shinano.

Nothing prevents unity with the One ... Verbiage! So much verbiage! Prose is a vehicle for mentation, intellection, thinking ... whatever you wish to call it. It slowly, methodically ploughs a field and thinks it has done a pretty good job. There's some shape to its achievement, a plan has been skilfully executed.

No such plan can exist for haiku, no such process, no such deliberation, or pacing or planning or toil. Haiku exists in a free unploughed, unploughable realm, virgin soil. Reflect on this...

Now, if you are ready to continue, watch the flowing and the merging in the following haiku:

> a cormorant
> glides close to the surface
> becoming grey sea

Tomislav Maretić
(Haiku from Croatia, trans. Djurdja V Rozic and Martin Lucas,
Blithe Spirit, Vol. 14, No.3, Sept. 2004)

This haiku could stand as a metaphor for what we mean by haiku enlightenment. The sea is not just the sea. It is the cosmic ocean. The only thing that is Real and Eternal. The cormorant/individual has sacrificed its notion of self by merging with the boundless ocean. This is where **Buddha** comes in: 'Enlightenment is straightly attained by freedom from separate selfhood.' Nothing prevents your unity with the One – nothing! – except the ego. (The **Buddha's** words are echoed in other traditions, 'I and the Father are One...')

So, the haikuist whose life is not altered by haiku is simply recording phenomena, as best (s)he can, but remains untouched, ungraced by the noumena, the hidden heart of all phenomena. And it always tells. So, what's to be done? Try harder? Not at all. No, the answer is nothing. Nothing is to be done. Nothing at all.

You want to be a somebody? Everybody wants to be a somebody. Try being a nobody. No, don't try. Just be. Be a NO BODY. Then, and only then, can haiku enlightenment riddle you to the core.

Why be a traitor to yourself or to haiku? **Issa** says (it may be apocryphal), 'The way of haiku and the way of Confucius and Buddha are the same in that if one forgets the true meaning of underlying principles and learns, in vain, only the form, he or she is a traitor...' (Quoted in *Pure Land Haiku: The Art of Priest Issa* by David G. Lanoue, Buddhist Books International, 2004).

So, do not be a traitor. Trust! **Swami Siddheswarananda** assures us, 'Realisation comes in search of us and we cannot go in search of Realisation...'

the far shore
drifting out of the mist
to meet us

> **Elizabeth Searle Lamb**
>
> (Quoted in *Zen Poems*, Ed Manu Bazzano, MQ
> Publications Ltd., 2002)

———

The **Baal Shem Tov** reminded his followers that the primordial spark exists in all things. We discover that spark in haiku:

heat shimmers:
the stone's soul
    still alive

> **Shiki**
> (Emiko Miyashita, *Shiki Haiku Calendar 2003*)

———

Know what haiku is now? Hopefully, if this is your first encounter, you will have a feeling for it by now. Don't lose that feeling! Who would have thought that something so apparently simple could be so elusive, so full? **R. H. Blyth** (in *Haiku*, Volume 1) writes: 'These are some of the characteristics of the state of mind which the creation and appreciation of haiku demand: Selflessness, Loneliness, Grateful Acceptance, Wordlessness, Non-Intellectuality, Contradictoriness, Humour, Freedom, Non-morality, Simplicity, Materiality, Love, and Courage.' Sounds like a lot, doesn't it? But some of these characteristics can begin to manifest themselves in all of us. How? By the very habit of haiku itself; those flashes of energising enlightenment – *kensho* – that accompany real haiku have the power to sustain the life of these characteristics in us and to conjure them at the required moment.

———

Look again ... Look through some of the haiku in this book. It may well be that you missed out on a few and that their full impact still awaits you. Do this now. Flick through the book again and keep the states mentioned by **Blyth** (above) in mind. You could write out all 13 on a sheet of paper. Armed with this list, make a random search now. How many of these characteristics, or others, can you find? Many excellent haiku create a space for more than one interpretation. They allow a space for you, the reader, to savour or even to complete the experience brilliantly hinted at.

Simple acts ... To write a haiku is a simple act. 'A real haiku's gotta be as simple as porridge and yet make you see the real thing,' we read in **Jack Kerouac's** *The Dharma Bums*. 'As simple as porridge.' That's good.

> evening coming—
> the office girl
> unloosing her scarf

Jack Kerouac

It is becoming increasingly difficult in our cluttered world to perform acts of utter simplicity. In *Turtle Island* (New Directions Publishing Corporation, 1974), **Gary Snyder** – the actual speaker (thinly disguised) speaking, above, in *The Dharma Bums* – sums it up:

> 'It is hard to even begin to gauge how much a complication of possessions, the notions of "my and mine", stand between us and a true, clear, liberated way of seeing the world. To live lightly on the earth, to be aware and alive, to be free of egotism, to be in contact with plants and animals, starts with simple concrete acts...'

What could be simpler than the act of haiku?

> water trough
> a horse
> drinking the sky

ai li
(*Blithe Spirit*, Vol. 8, No. 3, 1998)

---

inch by inch
through the trees
– the rising moon

Come, butter, come! This was a Celtic mantra, said when churning butter. How do we encourage the haiku moment, or our recognition of that concatenation of events that will give birth to a haiku? **Robert Spiess** gave stimulating advice to his many readers in America, and elsewhere, in the course of a long and productive life as a haikuist and editor:

'As haiku poets we should keep our sense perceptions open and relaxed, not using them forcefully to grasp experiences.' This is a wise observation, ignored at our peril. He goes on to say, 'With this almost detached way we do not block our inner awareness and intuition. Simultaneously we are then perceiving both inside and outside ourselves, so that these two conditions become a unity.' (*Modern Haiku*, Vol. 33. 3, Autumn 2002, Robert Spiess Memorial Issue)

Grateful for small mercies ... We are nearing the end of this journey – hopefully, for you, the beginning – on the haiku path. If nothing else, you will be, henceforth, grateful for small mercies:

> putting chopsticks aside—
> enough!
> thanks

> **Santōka**

Conclusion

A life-long encountering ... Through habitual reading and writing of haiku we can experience states of non-differentiation, of union with natural phenomena. Many people, if they think of this possibility at all, relegate such events to the lives of nature mystics and highly evolved spiritual poets. It need not be so. Along the haiku path, we encounter our own peculiar destiny. Compassion, intelligence, awareness, intuition, perspicacity and creativity are all fused and enlivened on the haiku path.

With frequent practice of haiku, our senses sharpen one another: as we watch and see more closely, the keener becomes our hearing, our sense of smell, until we are wordlessly brought into the great silence, the womb of creation where the haiku moment is born and reborn, spring, summer, autumn and winter. We acquire that 'singular state of mind', as French-language poet and critic, **Philippe Jaccottet**, describes it, which leads us to 'the peak of limpidity' and to 'the full and luminous life to which everybody aspires'. (Quoted in a review of the work of **R. H. Blyth**, English translation David Quin). This 'singular state of mind' is acquired through purifying consciousness, repeatedly, in haiku engagement:

> the empty rock pool—
> > till the mind clears,
> > > then a thousand little things

> > > > **Jim Norton**

Tagore wrote a letter in which he described a sensual union with all of creation: 'I felt that once upon a time I was at one with the rest of the earth, that grass grew green upon me, that the autumn sun fell on me and under its rays the warm scent of youth wafted from every pore of my far-flung evergreen body... ' The haiku path restores that sense of unity and non-duality which we all once enjoyed as our birthright; don't interpret this as a regression to infantile certainties, however. **Tagore** continues in the same vein: 'The current of my consciousness streams through each blade of grass, each sucking root, each sappy vein, and breaks out in the waving fields of corn and in the rustling leaves of the palms...' (*Rabindranath Tagore*, Krishna Dutta & Andrew Robinson, Rupa 2003).

In haiku, little details explode into life:

> the sparrow hops
> along the veranda
> with wet feet

Shiki
(R. H. Blyth)

An aura ... Good haiku have an aura, a shimmer, a glint. Apples on the table are just apples. When they become part of a still life by **Cézanne** they acquire life, an aura. What brings the aura to the apples – or what enhances their own aura – is the poet's glance.

Non-striving awareness ... Haiku is an open-eyed engagement with the word and with the world. It is not so much what paints itself on the retina as what resonates – through one or more of the senses – with the human spirit. Haiku moments, in all their purity, surprise us when – and only when – we have achieved passive, non-striving awareness:

> the moon
> above snow-capped mountains
> dropping hailstones

Sekitei Hara

Neither pro nor anti ... It is worth familiarising yourself with Chinese and Japanese classics, particularly the poetry of the T'ang Dynasty and the countless fables, parables, *koans* and poems that form part of the Zen tradition. Do not start on the haiku path with a pro-Zen or anti-Zen mentality. After all, Zen may be nothing more than a happy accident. It seems there were tremendous difficulties in translating Buddhist sutras from Sanskrit to Chinese. In many cases one was left with riddles, what appeared to be nothing more than runic rubbish. Meditating on these dark, sacred texts revealed no logic, no wisdom, no great revelation – thus the mind transcended meaning and therein found enlightenment in No-Mind! (One can look further into this theory in **Kogen Mizuno's** *Buddhist Sutras: Origin, Development, Transmission*, Tokyo: Kosei, 1982).

Seng-ts'an (known as **Sosan** in Japanese) was the Third Chinese Patriarch. He admonishes us, wisely: 'If you wish to know the truth, hold to no opinions – neither for nor against. Setting what you like against what you dislike, this is the disease of the mind.' Treasure this insight. If you can live by it, a thousand vistas will open up for you on the flowering haiku path.

Do not be alarmed by the possibility of ego-loss on this path. Do not be afraid! **Eugen Rosenstock-Huessy**, the German-American philosopher, reminds us that God is invisible; so, to be made in God's image is to be invisible! Don't be afraid of that either! The haiku is small enough – there isn't space in it for your ego. Leave your ego outside. You may return to it later (if you must!)

The conditioned mind ... Focusing on the here-and-nowness of the haiku moment, being in that moment, simply means that we facilitate the dissolving of the conditioned mind. (For more on the conditioned mind, try to get your hands on a book, or books, by **Raymond Karczewski**).

Haiku discipline results in our appreciation of a dazzling concatenation of events which otherwise might have remained beyond our ken:

> as it's swallowed
> a frog blinks
> in a snake's mouth

Itaru Ina
(*Modern Haiku*, Vol. 34.2, Summer 2003)

Haiku Enlightenment

The Gentle Art of Disappearing

Forgetting oneself is being enlightened by all things.

—Dōgen

Would you like to disappear? Haiku can show you the way!

'How painful it is to see people all wrapped up in themselves,' commented **Ryokan**. Well, it's unwrapping time, for all of us now, time to let go. How? Let's *see*!

Haiku is an ardent, inspired and inspiring engagement with everyday life, an intercourse with nature-centred events, mainly, events that are happening around us all of the time but which we perceive more keenly on the haiku path. Read true haiku with reverence, write true haiku – do it right and you can disappear, happily, now – and over and over again in the course of your life.

———

There's a professor in Chicago who has been studying happiness. What is happiness? It's all about flow, maintains **Mihaly Csikszentmihalyi** in *Finding Flow: The Psychology of Engagement with Everyday Life*: 'The metaphor of 'flow' is one that many people have used to describe the sense of effortless action they feel in moments that stand out as the best in their lives …'

———

Disappearing in the haiku moment … Think about moments of flow, ordinary or extraordinary events in your life in which you have experienced flow: it may have been entering another dimension while dancing, or when engaged in some aesthetic pursuit – music, pottery or painting; it may have been lovemaking, or the highlight of some athletic activity, or simply watching the dawn, or the stars, in some exotic location. You needn't shine as athlete, hill-walker or lover, no need to book a trip to Kerala or Kerry. You can flow now with haiku, like water, like a cloud.

Wandering monks were called *unsui* in Japan, literally 'cloud and water'. In Estonia, the perfection of life was personified in the singing wanderer: 'If you walk your path without singing then this is an insult to the land, to meadows and forests and trees, and they show their disapproval of such a wanderer by taking away from him the power of moving on…' (*Regilaul – music in our mother tongue* by **Mikk Sarv** *(Estonian Culture 1/2003 (1),* published by Estonian Institute).

———

Bashō moved about quite a bit and caught the beauty of flow and stillness, the intermingling textures of life:

The squid seller's call
mingles with the voice
of the cuckoo

Bashō
(*Matsuo Basho, Poems*, trans. Robert Hass, 2004)

It is your static, self-conscious, unflowing self which makes you so stolidly visible, so permanently present to others and to yourself. Disappear for a while. True haikuists will show you the way because they have developed a magnetic capacity to attract the haiku moment. What is the haiku moment? Nothing more than an alchemic mingling and fusion of essences in which you disappear. Become the cloud! Become the water, the breeze that moves them! The voice of a bird. **D. H. Lawrence** once remarked that in the beginning was the Chirp!

———

Do not resist ... Among the definitions of 'flow' in *Chambers Twentieth Century Dictionary*, we find: 'To run, as water: to move or change form like a fluid ... to melt...' All the sages, ancient and contemporary, are unanimous in praise of flowingness:

Do not resist
The journey's flow
And you will find yourself at One
With the mysterious unity of the Universe . . .

Chuang Tzu

———

Disappearing in the flame ... Mystics will show you what true haikuists already know:

'I, the fiery life of divine essence, am aflame beyond the beauty of the meadows, I gleam in the waters, and I burn in the sun, moon and stars... I awaken everything to life.'

It was **Hildegard von Bingen** who uttered those magnificent words. What a haikuist she would have made, had she known of the technique, given her life-long engagement with the secret life of plants and stones. Another German mystic, **Angelus Silesius**, was a master of minimalist verse; though

100

his strange couplets are generally too abstract to resemble haiku, he presents us with a fine, if cryptic, reason for disappearing:

> God, whose love and joy are present everywhere,
> Can't come to visit you unless you aren't there!

Angelus Silesius

Are you all wrapped up?

> Only to the extent that a person
> exposes his or her self
> over and over again
> to annihilation
> can that which is
> indestructible
> arise
> within themselves . . .

Karlfried Graf Dürckheim
(*The Way of Transformation*)

So, we hear this message from all sides, in many cultures, East and West, down through the ages. We cannot ignore it. The true haikuist cannot ignore it. It is his life's breath.

———

frosty morning
     a robin bares his breast
to the whole world

Disappearing in the ordinary ... Haiku poems focus on ordinary, seasonal goings on around us. Some form of brain synchronization happens in the haiku moment and the ordinary becomes extraordinary. We do not need a magic wand, or magic mushrooms, to disappear. A turnip can take us there, a tree, a crow, a shadow on a lake, the hissing of geese.

Meher Baba reminds us: 'The best way to cleanse the heart and prepare for the stilling of the mind is to lead a normal, worldly life .'

> *i m'aonar anocht*
> *leis na torbáin*
> *leis an gcruinne*

alone tonight
  with the tadpoles
    with the universe
GR

in the silver dewdrops
vanishing…
my house

Issa

(David G. Lanoue)

The haikuist can disappear first thing in the morning, last thing at night, each haiku moment being a cleansing of the heart, a stilling of the mind, a vanishing. Where is the sane man or woman who, deep down, desires an unclean heart, an unstilled mind?

———

Disappearing in light ... The haikuist's focus is such that the interconnectedness of all things becomes radiantly apparent. The Mexican poet **José Juan Tablada**, who visited Japan, was one of the first Westerners to cultivate haiku:

tierno saúce
casi oro, casi ámbar,
casi lúz

slight willow
almost gold, almost amber,
almost light

José Juan Tablada

The effortless action of becoming, which is manifested a thousand times over in the daily world around us, was intuited in **Tablada's** timeless haiku moment. And where is he? He has disappeared into the willow. Its lambent willowness.

Rumi says:

> Open the window of your bosom
> Let the spirits fly in and out . . .

Rumi

True haiku is an opening to an experience of freedom, fluency, spontaneity, a sharing of light.

Angelus Silesius, in another of his immortal couplets, says:

> *Freund, so du etwas bist, so bleib doch ja nicht stehn:*
> *Man muss aus einem Licht fort in das andre gehn*

> Friend, whatever you are, you must not stand still:
> One must from one light into the other spill

Angelus Silesius

Zen-Haiku Master, **James W. Hackett**, in his *A Traveler's Haiku* (Hokuseido, 2004) offers us this:

> clinging to a twig
> now full of nothing but light—
> the end of summer

J. W. Hackett

Everything disappears ... One could say that everything disappears, or will one day:

> day after day
> bits of the chained bicycle
> disappear

Annie Bachini
(*Presence #9*)

From self-infatuation to selflessness ... One is grossly visible in the world – to the world and to oneself – when one suffers from self-infatuation, self-engrossment, self-importance. Haiku is a streaming into the light in which self-infatuation cannot exist. The pure and purifying action of the haiku moment causes us to dissolve into another dimension. And who or what are we then? Creatures of light. Nothing more. Nothing less. And though we may return to the chiaroscuro of life, we are changed. We have, briefly, known our brilliant nature. The self has been sloughed and only Self remains.

> faint sunlight
> injecting the veins
> of a falling leaf
>
> **GR**

he will not desert her!
a bat
circling the moon
Gyôdai

The melting of rigidity ... The haiku path is one of playful light, of love, of joy. As **Sharon Salzberg** teaches us in *Loving-Kindness – The Revolutionary Art of Happiness*: 'Without the rigidity of concepts, the world becomes transparent and illuminated, as though lit from within. With this understanding, the interconnectedness of all that lives becomes very clear. We see that nothing is stagnant and nothing is fully separate...' The haiku path breaks down 'rigidity of concepts' and the world becomes illumined.

Indeed, were it not for this transparency, this inner luminescence, this interconnectedness, the haiku moment could not exist for us mortals at all and, so, it would be impossible for us to disappear in its clarity.

In many good haiku we spy a 'miniature animated cosmos', to borrow an apt phrase from **Octavio Paz**:

> out come the creepy crawlies
> all over the earth
> see? they have shadows
>
> **Kuge**

Disappearing in the garden ... Even maggots and beetles are part of the eternal flow. There is very little out there which does not possess *mononoke,* nature energy.

Some haikuists may need to learn how to disappear, initially, in a wood, on an unruffled lake, on top of a mountain, out on the rolling sea, or simply by visiting a splendid garden. **Ken Wilbur** has noticed how a great garden can 'pull the sensitive viewer out of him- or herself and into the garden, so completely that the separate self-sense disappears entirely and at least for a brief moment one is ushered into a nondual and timeless awareness.' This is a good way for the apprentice haikuist to get an inkling of the quality of the haiku moments awaiting him/her.

Once you experience the disappearance of 'the separate self-sense' you will know how haiku can authenticate this experience for you, over and over again.

Find a garden, then, and bring the haiku masters with you, the Sufi poets, or the timeless couplets of **Silesius:**

> *Die Seel, ein ewger Geist, ist über alle Zeit:*
> *Sie lebt auch in der Welt schon in der Ewigkeit*

> The soul, an eternal spirit, is beyond time's hold:
> Even in this world it is in eternity's fold

Angelus Silesius

Silesius also said *Die Zeit ist Ewigkeit, Ewigkeit ist Zeit*/Time is Eternity, Eternity is Time. **Wu-men** (1183 –1260) stated the same thing:

> One instant is eternity
> Eternity is the now . . .

Wu-men

If we miss out on this insight we cannot experience the tremendous explosion necessary to disappear.

—◦◦◦—

Disappearing in sound ... As the haikuist's art deepens, magnificent gardens, mountains and gorges will become totally unnecessary. The haikuist will disappear anywhere, in a shallow brook, a sewer, in a steaming dunghill! Alchemists call this a distillation.

106

Even in great cities, New York or Baghdad, we can disappear: 'feel the delight/ of walking in the noisy streets/ and being the noise' **(Rumi)**. We can see a similarity here with disappearing into music. The Fuke sect in Japan used the bamboo flute (*shakuhachi*) to enter into a state of absolute sound known as *tettei on*. They had a saying: 'Become a Buddha in one sound.' What kind of a sound is that? It is the sound heard in mountain streams, waterfalls, rapids and cascades by the great, wandering haikuist **Santōka** and even, one suspects, a sound heard as he urinated on weeds.

In haiku – one-breath poetry – we can disappear into a buddhafield. What is to hold us back? The city? The woods? The forests? The flowers? The clouds? The rain? The mountains?

> amidst the deep mountains
> on my hat
> only the sound of falling leaves

Kikusha-ni
(*Japanese Women Artists* by **Patricia Fister**, Spencer Art Museum, 1988)

> a summer storm
> each and every raindrop
> bearing its own sound

Robert Bebek

> their hungry cry
> carried away by clouds
> to where there are no gulls

GR

And silence ...

> more silent than the hour
> before stars awake
> silence of the cats

GR

Laurence Sterne says, 'Eloquence does not arise from a laboured and far-fetched elocution, but from a surprising mixture of simplicity and majesty.'

This simplicity and majesty is often found among the so-called unlettered members of society and in the oral literatures of the world.

Listen to the Elders…As you perfect the art of reading and writing haiku, the wisdom of the elders will become manifestly clear. The Ojibway taught us this: 'My son! A lone wolf is rarely found in the wild. Wolves are social creatures like you and me. Just as you watch over your sister, so does a wolf watch over his brother. Just as you listen to your father, so does the wolf listen to his mother. Just as our family eats together, so too does the wolf. My son! Our people and the wolves are the same.'

becoming a cow
would be fine – morning naps
and the evening cool

Shikō
(*A Haiku Menagerie*)

jumping back in the pond
what only yesterday
    was a tadpole

Longing to disappear ... There seems to be a deep longing in the human spirit to disappear – that is to say, to know its own nature.. The great Portuguese poet **Fernando Pessoa** says, 'Fly, bird, fly away, teach me how to disappear!'

This longing becomes manifest early on, in the games of childhood, in hide and seek. Do we miss those games as adults? Did we ever truly understand their significance? 'Nature loves to hide,' said **Heraclitus**.

A red crab
hiding in the sand—
pure waters

> **Fukuda Kodojin**
> *(Old Taoist: The Life, Art and Poetry of Fukuda Kodojin (1865 –1944)* Stephen Addiss with Jonathan Chaves, Columbia University Press, 1999)

a winter squall
hid in the bamboos
and lost itself

> **Bashō**
> *(Noel Griffin)*

—ᴧᴧ—

Playful innocence ... The haiku moment is a disappearance into the playful, innocent world of childhood. One may ask, was it ever that innocent? Did it not always suggest the possibility of pain and fear, reinforced by fairy tales that bristled with ogres and wolves? Is the innocence we associate with childhood some form of intense longing in mankind for an Eden, a Utopia that may or may not have existed?

One way or the other, the innocence of childhood has always been threatened, by slave labour, by sexual and other forms of abuse, by hunger and disease and even, in certain parts of the world today, by children's armies. And yet, it is possible to restore lost innocence, by disappearing into the haiku moment, the spirit which is endless, unborn, eternal.

only a half-squawk
from the crow—
but what a chorus it sets off

> **GR**

110

A second before, or a second afterwards, and this haiku moment would not have existed. But such haiku moments can happen frequently, several times a day. And as we dip into their purity – their singularity or the concatenation of events which they can fire – are we not momentarily released from the burdens of responsibility and rationality, from sins real or imagined, and plunged, fearlessly, into the cleansing flow of things?

We never really lost our ability to be delighted and surprised by the colour, taste, sound, odour and texture of things. We may think we did, we may feel we did, but the haiku moment brings it all back. We begin to see again, as we once saw:

> around the eyes
> of the old fisherman
> permanent ripples

> **George Swede**
> (*Almost Unseen*, Brooks Books 2000)

You Are A Star!

> Man is not body. The heart, the spirit, is man.
> and this spirit is an entire star out of which he is built.
> If therefore a man is perfect in his heart,
> nothing in the whole light of Nature
> is hidden from him.

> **Paracelsus**

For many people, the desire to disappear is mere escapism. Take, for instance, the largest group of foreigners in Japan, Koreans known as Zainichi. They are under constant pressure to conform. Their cultural and linguistic identity becomes brittle. (See *Japanese Society* by **Yoshio Sugimoto**, Cambridge University Press, 1997).

One of these Koreans, **Kidong Kang,** uses haiku to express his desire to flee the very home of haiku itself:

> swallow left behind
> makes me want to fly
> Zainichi me

> **Kidong Kang**
> (quoted in *Modern Haiku*, Winter-Spring 2004)

Bob Dylan says he likes to disappear because it's not good being too conspicuous. He says **Christ** was too conspicuous and they crucified him. Everything today is far too conspicuous, in one's face. A million times less would be too much. We can learn from the old fox:

> concealing his tail
> among heads of barley
> old fox

Tesshi

———

Most adults no longer know how to disappear. There was a man who only passed away a few years ago in Conamara and he had the *Ortha na Dofheictheachta* (the Charm for Disappearing). He could go through a village with his donkey and cart, carrying a keg of illicit spirits, and having uttered the *ortha* there wasn't a policeman on earth or a spy-satellite in the sky that was capable of spotting him. Or so they say…

———

Mad monk disappears … Boating is also conducive to the gentle art of disappearance. As **Thoreau** reflected: 'Sometimes as I drift on Walden Pond I cease to exist and begin to be…' The eccentric monk **Ikkyu** compressed incredible energy into astounding poems and beautiful haiku. This energy came from disappearing into the void. He too was drifting, on Lake Biwa, near Kyoto, when suddenly – Caaaaaaaaaaaaaaaaw! – a crow shatters the silence and **Ikkyu** disappears in boundless *satori*.

The same crow might have had no effect whatsoever on him a few seconds earlier or a few seconds later. Disappearing happens unexpectedly, out of the blue. It's a type of spontaneous combustion. Another lake, combining stillness, movement and sound:

> across the still lake
> through upcurls of morning mist—
> the cry of a loon

O Mabson Southard
(*The Haiku Anthology*, Ed. **Cor van den Heuvel**, W.W. Norton, 1999)

And nowhere is the poet to be seen!

Lakes, mountains, ruins … Lake districts are not strictly necessary for haiku poets. Sure, some of them like to hang around ruins or disappear in strange landscapes:

> bluebells among ruins
> the nameless fields
> beyond

Seán Mac Mathúna

The poignancy of history emerges here, memory and loss of memory. With language shift (from Irish to English,) and with massive emigration, considerable areas of landscape lost or changed their identity and name; and lost, too, was all the lore and legend surrounding the names. Paradoxically, the above haiku also shows us life amid decay; the last word of the haiku seems to bring us to an area that transcends the vicissitudes of time and history. We disappear into the 'beyond'.

We cannot see the whole world. We see it in haikuful glimpses:

> *aşteptând eclipsa*
> *un pahar cu vin roşu*
> *pentru fiecare*

> awaiting the solar eclipse
> a glass of red wine
> for everyone

Ion Codrescu
(*Mountain Voices*, Ami-Net 2000)

We see the world – in Catalonia (where the Romanian haikuist was at the time) or, next, in Japan – in its moment-to-moment becoming:

> water spiders
> big and little rings
> may be a family

Fujino Sunao
(*Haiku International, 1995*)

A becoming world of miraculous interconnectedness:

> persimmons getting soft
> day by day
> more birds

> **Iwakoshi Seifū**
> *(ibid.)*

—◦◦◦—

More birds ... Our haiku would be limited or deficient in many ways if we saw birds as mere pleasant, aerial acrobats, their singing nothing but sweetness. Birds are also rapacious.

The **Buddha**'s quest for enlightenment really began not when he first witnessed those things previously veiled from him – pampered prince as he was – namely suffering, disease and death; his quest subconsciously commenced on witnessing the royal ritual of spring ploughing, birds of various species squabbling for food, for worms and grubs that were invisible before the red earth was turned. So, in haiku, all aspects of nature, and our own, are revealed. And becoming-ness is celebrated for its mystery:

> how a brook so small
> becomes in its wanderings
> a pathway for stars

> **Foster Jewell**
> *(Passing Moments,* 1974)

—◦◦◦—

You can disappear anywhere! **Chang Chiu-ch'en** was in the toilet when he heard the croak of a frog piercing the universe, turning the whole world into a single family!

The transparency of pure haiku can enter our lives, informing and transfiguring the invisible warp and woof of our selves:

> some of the sails
> become transparent
> in the spring mist

> **Konagai Kazuko**
> *(ibid.)*

114

Angelic moments ... We disappear because pure haiku are not authored by us: they are mediated through us once we become invisible. Each pure haiku that arises from a deep, genuine haiku moment is an unravelling of our physicality, through the seen towards the unseen, from the part to the whole, from little details to the invisible order that holds the universe together.

These angelic moments do not simply describe cute or pretty scenes found in juvenile pseudo-haiku. Nor are these angelic moments some sensitive re-imagining or re-fashioning of works of nature by the fanciful mind. These angelic moments are what they are – an experience of the freedom, the swiftness, the grace and the wisdom of angels. This grace reflects the light of seasons, the moods of seasons, the time of the day ... in the play of light itself, nature in its frolicsome state, in wistfulness, in all its grandeur of sights and sounds and in its immense silence.

Everything that is out there is also within. One might say there is a cosmos without and a cosmos within. In the haiku moment they are drawn together as one, each and every time. And, over time, the distinction becomes less and less. What a great gift is this grace we call haiku. Do accept it.

—◦∿◦—

Haiku and non-haiku ... Strictly speaking, there are no bad or mediocre haiku. There are only excellent haiku – and non-haiku. A woman is pregnant or she is not. A haiku is pregnant or it is not. Strictly speaking, there are no first prizes, simply haiku that qualify and those that do not. Haikuists who understand this are incapable of envy or jealousy: good haiku, from whatever source, fill them with amazement and admiration, be the subject a mouse or a mountain. Squabbles in the haiku community – or in any community – are indicative of not enough disappearing going on!

Do we know what we see? Seeing is truly a mystery. **Hans Magnus Enzensberger** has a couplet:

> *Mach die Augen auf und das Erscheinende ist verschwunden*
> *Mach die Augen zu und das Verschwundene erscheint*

> Open your eyes and that which appeared has vanished
> Close your eyes and that which vanished appears

Hans Magnus Enzensberger

—◦∿◦—

féach! dúchas na gaoithe
á ghabháil chuige féin
ag crann

look! a tree
is becoming the spirit
of the wind

Disappearing in the game ... There should always be a certain playfulness and sprightliness in our lives, if we are to disappear. The word "play" itself is hidden in the word haiku. Hindus speak of Leela, "cosmic play". In the West we speak of Homo Ludens. Haiku can be our game. Not a competitive game, mind you. Think of it in terms outlined by **Meher Baba**:

> 'To penetrate into the essence of all being and significance, and to release the fragrance of that inner attainment for the guidance and benefit of others, by expressing in the world of forms – truth, love, purity and beauty – this is the sole game that has any intrinsic and absolute worth.'

—///—

Disappearing with the birds ... In a profile of larger-than-life travel-writer **Redmond O'Hanlon** (*The Guardian, Review*, 8. 11. 03), **Andrew Brown** says of bird-watching: 'To watch them with the right devoted attention brings on a sort of ecstasy in which the unwinged world recedes.' Yes indeed, and the haikuist who brings 'the right devoted attention' to his craft discovers a pristine quality in the living world in which, Adam-and-Eve-like, things are seen and named for the first time:

> on the tip of the
> newly sprouted bamboo . . .
> a baby sparrow
>
> **Issa**
> *(David G. Lanoue)*

Yes, the successful haiku is truly a fine balancing-act!

> lake   goose
>
> gooselake
>
> Lake Goose
>
> **GR**

> sitting in air
> a crow on something
> snowed on
>
> **Raymond Roseliep**
> (*Global Haiku, Twenty-Five Poets World-wide*, Ed. George
> Swede & Randy Brooks, Iron Press & Mosaic Press, 2000)

117

By 'right devoted attention' to haiku we mean a pointed attentiveness which, paradoxically, is also an emptying of the mind, allowing the thousand things – as **Dōgen** refers to phenomena – to enter our sphere of consciousness:

> the alchemist bee
>   nothing on its mind
>   but liquid gold
>
> **GR**

—⁓—

Stepping back ... It is when the self steps back, withdraws unconditionally, in the haiku moment – and in that moment's spontaneous, immediate (or subsequent) re-creation in words – only then does the universe begin to appear. We must disappear to allow its appearance.

Naturalist **W H Hudson** reminds us: 'Unless the soul goes out to see what we see we do not see it; nothing do we see, not a beetle, not a blade of grass.' Every haikuist worth his salt knows this from experience.

Those who see the small are called clear-headed,
Those who hold to gentleness are called strong

Lao Tzu

When you rest in quietness and your image of yourself fades,
and your image of the world fades,
and your ideas of others fade, what's left?
A brightness, a radiant emptiness that is simply what you are . . .

Adyashanti

> a church spire only
>   through the mist
>   a wingless silence
>
> **GR**

—⁓—

The way of unobtrusiveness ... With so much violence, poverty, hunger and injustice in the world, with languages in decay and all their accumulated treasures of songs and sayings dying with them, species after species being wiped out, so many broken homes, broken hearts, what gives us the right to enjoy quiet moments with haiku? This: haiku teaches us to be unobtrusive, to walk lightly, invisibly, in this world. It may not be too fanciful to claim, as some do, in relation to the rise of global haiku on the internet and the proliferation of haiku exchanges via e-mail, that such activity performs a virtual *harae* or cleansing of the world's *kegare* or pollution; such purification has always been an integral part of Shinto ritual.

By its very size, the haiku cultivates an empathy with all things similarly small, all things struggling to live and to breathe and to flower. (If asked to opt for **Thomas Jefferson's** "bigger is better" or **E. F. Schumacher's** "small is beautiful", what would you say?)

By flowering in haiku consciousness, we contribute to a fragrance which makes the world bearable and our lives liveable. The act of haiku is uncompromisingly compassionate.

> leaving them alone
> moonlight
> on roses

ai li

(*Cold Morning. An International haiku anthology*, ed. Margaret Saunders, Hamilton Haiku Press, Canada, 1998)

Santōka saw beauty even in a miserable coin thrown his way, a small coin with barely any purchase value:

> the glint
> from a little coin
> thrown my way

Santōka

The dynamic of the successful haiku is such that choice language matches succinctness of form, creating just the right touch, the right tone, to escape the clichéd, chocolate-box cover it could so easily have been.

By using the intrusive 'I' as seldom as possible, the haikuist can become spectral, invisible, universal, of the same essence as the moonlight, the glint of a thrown coin.

Haiku for its own sake … We live in a world obsessed with profit and loss, a world in which our actions are expected to show some gain, some material usefulness. Disappearing in the haiku moment might seem, therefore, to be a form of sacrilege. How does it honour the god of our age, Mammon?

There is an interesting story about a Christian missionary in China. No doubt he was sincere enough in what he was trying to achieve but, as often happens, he was finding it difficult to come to terms with the niceties of an ancient civilization. Out on a contemplative stroll, he comes across a Chinese priest chanting in a temple. Curious as to know what exactly this was all about, when the chanting stops the missionary approaches the priest. 'To whom were you praying just now?' he asks. The Chinese priest is puzzled. Strange questions these missionaries ask, he thinks. 'To whom was I praying? To no one at all,' comes the honest reply. The missionary is stumped. To no one at all? How can this be? 'Well then, tell me please,' he enquires, 'for what were you praying?' Again, the Chinese priest is taken aback. He answers plainly: 'For what was I praying? For nothing.' The missionary looks at him. Is this fathomable? For nothing? He purses his lips. There's nothing much to be gained here, he says to himself, and makes as if to leave. The priest calls after him. The missionary turns, thinking to himself, 'What next?' The Chinese priest smiles. 'And there was no one praying, you know.'

Haiku reaches its purest form in such purposelessness and egolessness: grace for no other purpose but grace itself. By sloughing off all concepts, all preconceptions, all judgments and fashions, by burning the furniture of the mind, the haikuist becomes disinterested – which is not to say aloof. 'Disinterested contemplation of nature and art brings about a state of mind which is universal in that it can transcend the individual ego,' says **Anna Bonshek** in *Mirror of Consciousness, Art, Creativity and Veda* (Motilal Banarsidass Publishers, 2001). Let us always keep the universality of haiku in mind. It now belongs to the world.

My starting point is
the fundamental initial fact
that each one of us
is perforce linked
by all material organic and psychic strands
of his being
to all
that surrounds him . . .

Teilhard de Chardin

—ᴧᴧᴧ—

120

Reminder ... If you haven't taken a pause recently, do so now. Or flick back through the pages. Did you read a haiku that impressed you or astonished you? If so, does it still impress you? Can you say why?

Are you beginning to have faith in haiku? Or do you suspect that the wool is being pulled over your eyes? There are many deceptions in the world. But haiku is not one of them. Make up your own mind. But first, give your mind another rest while remembering that it is not mind but the temporary absence of mind which will facilitate your disappearance.

Shri Ranjit Maharaj says: 'Go deep in yourself, so deep that you disappear.'

———

Deep ecology ... All the creepy crawlies of this world, the bugs and insects and worms, all have their place and their function in deep ecology. When we begin to notice the vibrancy of the microcosm close to hand, we learn to appreciate the grandeur – and the frailty – of the macrocosm and man's place in the larger picture.

Enjoying quiet moments with haiku does not mean reclining on a rose-scented divan – it is noticing the smallest things as they go into hibernation, or emerge. The haikuist utters the canticle of all creatures:

> morning breeze
> in the hairs
> of a caterpillar

Buson

And how lovely that it's morning! This is a true wake-up-call haiku.

———

self-encounter—
cautious deer
in shallow water

féin-teagmháil—
fianna aireacha
sa tanalacht

In early 2004, the CBS Evening News ran a series called *Man V. Nature*. Versus! Mountain lions, alligators … all out to get you. Around about the same time the Pentagon was warning about the threat of global warming. We've got it wrong. Haiku is a way back to sanity and wholeness.

Disappearing in the haiku moment is to re-appear refreshed and re-energised in this floating world:

> *vrbe na obali*
> *kap pokap jutarnje rose*
> *pada u reku*

> willows by the riverbank—
> drop by drop of morning dew
> falling into the river

> **Dušan Mijajlović Adski**
> (*A Jug for Dew*, Punta, 2002)

As in **Tablada**'s willow-haiku earlier on, there is more happening here than meets the eye. Drop by drop is suggestive of the flow of time. Are we in the moment-to-moment flow or are we carried along by it, unconsciously?

—ᴧᴧᴧ—

Taken by surprise … The haiku moment is perceived in the present but, of course, the dew becomes the river, eventually to join the seas, the winds, the rains and, in evaporation, the whole process of existence begins anew, out of the past, into the present and beyond. The discerning and witnessing of the naturalness and the meaningfulness of such cycles is one of the important gifts of haiku.

> vanishing
> in heat shimmers . . .
> the simple hut

> **Issa**

Issa was only too well aware of how everything and everyone eventually disappears – even loved ones before their time. Heat shimmers are heat shimmers. They may not be particularly attractive to every eye. But the haikuist presents them and their actions as an event, a significant haiku event. And how can we ever tire of these manifestations, if we are truly alive?

If we lose the capacity to be surprised, we forfeit the deep core of our humanity. Let us remind ourselves that for the Greeks, *thaumazein* – wonder – was the beginning of all philosophy.

Wonder is the title of a poem by the wonderful **Thomas Traherne** in which he says:

> I within did flow
> With seas of life, like wine;
> I nothing in the world did know
>   But 'twas divine.

Thomas Traherne

This is the epitaph of every successful life, the alpha and omega of a haikuist's span on earth.

―∽∿∾―

Flowing to a stop ... The poet has mentioned one of our key-words, 'flow'; did you notice? Flow is the essential haiku ingredient, the happiness ingredient, the life-stuff. We can also flow towards a momentary stop:

> gazing so long
> at the clock – something inside me
> comes to a stop

Lucian Suciu
(*Knots: An Anthology of Southeastern European Haiku Poetry,* Ed. Dimitar Anakiev *and* Jim Kacian*, 1999*)

―∽∿∾―

Infusion ... Infusion in the other is the key to disappearing in the haiku moment. **Osho** used to say it was a bit like sex. It is, in a way, except that celibates can do it. An unsung poet, **Govinda Krishna Chettur**, says:

You are the Rose of me,
In you have I lost myself, utterly . . .

Govinda Krishna Chettur
(*The Golden Treasury of Indo-Anglian Poetry*,
New Delhi, 1970)

―᭡᭡᭡―

Becoming invisible ... When we talk here about disappearing, it is not something out of *The Invisible Man.* This is not science fiction. **Robert Spiess,** a prophet of modern haiku, speculated thus: 'The relation of the poet to a now-moment of awareness that will be the basis of a haiku should be like water pouring into water...' What haiku was he reading at the time? This one by **Bashō**, perhaps?

pouring the hot day
into the sun
the River Mogami

Bashō

―᭡᭡᭡―

Flow and merge ... the way of disappearing ... In many countries, from Ireland to India, rivers are deities, goddesses. Not surprisingly, there are many classical scriptural references to rivers and their flow:

As the rivers flowing east and west
Merge in the sea and become one with it,
Forgetting they were ever separate rivers,
So do all creatures lose their separateness
When they merge at last into pure Being

Chandogya Upanishad

―᭡᭡᭡―

The River of Time ... Zen-Haiku Master **James W. Hackett** tells us about another river: 'In India, millions of pilgrims continue to revere the Ganges as the world's most holy river. Meanwhile *Time*, life's most sacred stream, flows inexorably on, seldom reverenced or even regarded, save for an enlightened few.'

a corpse
in the Ganges
a crow takes a ride

GR

In the flowingness of air and water and wind we can learn what our own true nature is. As **Langston Hughes** wrote in *The Negro Speaks of Rivers* (1921):

I've known rivers:
Ancient, dusky rivers.
My soul has grown deep like the rivers . . .

Langston Hughes

—⁓—

Merge and flow ... This is how to disappear... Glorious as many scriptures are, true haiku can rival them or surpass them in beauty by *showing*, not merely *telling*, by dynamic, physical expression of transcendental experience, as opposed to lofty speculation and obtuse terminology.

—⁓—

A Samoan vision ... Well, we have encountered a number of rivers above, one in Eastern Europe, another in Japan, the Ganges, the reference to rivers in general from the Upanishads, the rivers in the poem by **Hughes** and **Hackett**'s river of time. Where do you live? Most cities are founded on rivers. You live on a street, more than likely. Wouldn't it be interesting to see what the idea of a street must have felt like to a Samoan chief a mere 100 years ago?

Tuiavii says: 'The Papalagi (white people) live like a sea mussel in fixed housing. They live between stones, like centipedes between cracks of lava...' It looks like the wise chief was anticipating the once-popular song 'Little Boxes', doesn't it? 'And they're all made out of ticky-tacky and they all look just the same!'

The chief goes on to describe how he imagines our dwellings: 'These boxes of stone are grouped together closely in large numbers, no tree, no bush separates them ... at a distance of a stone's throw, at the other side, there is an equal series of boxes of stone ... between both rows

126

there is just a narrow crack, called "street" by the Papalagi. This crack is often as long as a river and covered with hard stones…'

Chief Tuiavii
(Recorded by Erich Scheurmann)

Chief Tuiavii preached a good sermon to his people and we, whether Papalagi or not, should take note: not to be obdurate, to be fluid, free, not to be encased, to find inspiration in the sun, the breeze, the swelling oceans, the soaring birds, the vanishing clouds, not to be dictated to by that little thing which we wear on our wrist, something that calculates what **Tuiavii** has heard we call 'time'. And time draws our consciousness into the future, away from the now, into an unnatural flow. What time is it? Oh, an important meeting at three.

Osho, who may not always have lived as wisely as he spoke, wisely said: 'If you are in the future, then ego seems to be very substantial. If you are in the present the ego is a mirage, it starts disappearing.'

―ᴧᴧᴧ‒

Haiku is a powerful time-stopper. The haiku moment cannot be measured by time, or bound by time. It is outside of time. As such, it is a sacred moment. **Ellen Davis** could have been talking about the uniqueness of the haiku moment when she said: 'The sacred moment lives outside of time and therefore it cannot judge, for it has no past or future to compare itself to.'

―ᴧᴧᴧ‒

Those who think haiku is something slight, something artificial, should think again. True haiku moments are sacred. **Bede Griffiths** noted how a lot of the time we feverishly anticipate some imagined excitement:

'We have to learn to step back from this into the freedom and possibility of the present.'

November maples—
cascade of crimson
anointing the dawn

Myrna Sloam

What could be more sacred than to use the syllables of a mantra to count fish:

NA-MU-A-MI-DA
the way my dead mother
counted her sardines

Tsuruta Kyōko
(Haiku International 1995)

—◠◠◠—

Non-grasping ...

cranes left
without taking
anything

Kida Senjo
(Haiku International 1995)

The sensibility of pure haiku can be perceived in this exquisite observation of the cranes. Let us call it the 'non-grasping' effect. The birds disappear. They have taken nothing, not a berry, not a grain of rice. The nature of ego is grasping, craving, desiring. The nature of egolessness is non-grasping, non-craving – pure witness.

What has caused the wars we have known in our time? Grasping.

—◠◠◠—

Collapse of territoriality ... In the sacred moment in which haiku is conceived and born, the haikuist is no longer grossly visible to himself or others. What comes into his sphere of vision is not shooed away as an intruding presence, or grasped selfishly, rather it is contemplated freely with all the senses. Territoriality collapses in sharing, in silent music – *la musica callada* of **John of the Cross**...

silence—
the sound of a bird walking
on scattered leaves

Ryūshi

pomlando jutro
zgodnje ptice zobljejo
tanko tišino

spring morning
early birds are pecking
the thin silence

Silva Mizerit

(*SEASONS, The Magazine of the Haiku Club of Slovenia*, Autumn/Winter 2005 No. 28/29)

We know, or should know, that wars have been about territoriality, spheres of influence, geo-political strategies. We cannot end wars until we have the mind and the disposition of **Ryūshi**, so that all things, from centipedes to quadrupeds to bipeds can walk unthreatened on the earth.

Might there be something in a name, some inherent quality in our given name that shapes who we become? It would seem that the name '**Ryushi**' suggests versatility and spontaneity. Flow!

When the notion of territoriality and tribalism begins to implode on itself, then home is anywhere, everywhere. After all, if you know anything about geology, where your little country – or continent – appears on the map is not where it was, or what it was, some billions of years ago.

with every gust
the butterfly finds a new home
on the willow

Bashō

(Noel Griffin)

⤳⤳⤳

Distinctions flow and become fluid ...

opening their hearts
ice and water
are friends again

Teishitsu

⤳⤳⤳

What effect does haiku have on the world? We can only guess. Each true haiku brings a little more clarity and harmony into the world and global haiku today increases this possibility:

One after another
as the birds dip their sharp beaks—
water-rings of spring

Katō Kokō

(Four Seasons: Haiku Anthology Classified by Season Words,
Ed. Kokō Katō, Kō Poetry Association, 1991)

———~/v/v~———

Invisible words ... Sometimes, as the haikuist disappears, transported by the ineffable beauty or thusness or 'itness' of his surroundings, words disappear. One is in the world but lost to the world, lost for words. One must call upon words, recall their shape and sound, and there is a certain poignancy in all of this because what words can adequately convey the immensity of creation as it expresses itself in one revelation after another?

wow! . . . that's all
upon the blossom-covered
hills of Yoshino

Teishitsu

That's all, folks ... Perhaps a haiku such as this could not have appeared without the disappearance of many others: **Teishitsu** destroyed thousands of his haiku.

———~/v/v~———

Do not go to Yoshino ... Do not visit the hills of Yoshino – do not go anywhere – with the intention of writing a haiku. And don't copy the masters – that would be as boring as two halves of a melon, as **Bashō** warned. (Study the greats, by all means).

It has been pointed out in the *The Glowing Moment* that our preparations for the haiku moment will be foiled by intentionality. In his *Divine Beauty, The Invisible Embrace* (Bantam Press, 2003), **John O' Donohue** eloquently states: 'Beauty is a free spirit and will not be trapped within the grid of intentionality. In the light of beauty, the strategies of the ego melt like a web against a candle...'

If you go on a *ginko* or compositional stroll, be passively aware, that is all. Observe the appearance and reappearance of phenomena, and the half-hid:

Spring snowfall
on the tucked-in heads
of drifting sea birds

H. F. Noyes
(Four Seasons)

An insect living
in the stone animal's mouth—
time of melting snow

Katō Kenkō
(ibid)

When the art of reading true haiku develops, the reader, too, can momentarily disappear, into the colour of a leaf or a blossom:

plum blossoms—

red, red

red

Izen

Those who have looked at **Izen**'s original Japanese detect a note of idiocy in the diction. One way of dropping out of blue-collar, white-collar or collarless society is to become a 'holy fool'. But only through wisdom can such foolishness be acquired.

———

And into colourlessness ...

after the storm
fog off the sea
curling into snail shells

Seán Mac Mathúna

Into an absence ...

> the lake smoothes over
> and that loon
> still hasn't come back up

David Elliott
(*ibid.*)

Let's have a World Haiku Day and all disappear at once! It would ease some of the world's weight, its stony gravity.

—⁓—

sickle moon—

      reaping

            emptiness

Kabir vanishes ... The great Indian poet, **Kabir** (1398 – 1518), did a famous vanishing act. His Hindu followers longed to claim him after his death. He was theirs. His Muslim followers wished to do the same. Didn't he belong to them? Scuffles broke out. But to whom did **Kabir** belong? The Hindus? The Muslims?

On lifting his death-shroud they discovered that the poet's body had disappeared. Nothing left but a bunch of flowers. A scent. Maybe he was trying to tell us something?

Santōka advised us not to care a fig for the fashions, follies and figurations of the times we live in. He composed his haiku 'in a state of mind and body cast off'.

Today's world is constantly in search of the latest thing, the latest fashion or fad, the latest diet, the latest label, the new kid on the block. This craving, this dis-ease, is really an incapacity to view everything – absolutely everything – as new.

Shiki told his disciple **Kyoshi**: 'If you examine a moonflower closely your previous mental images will completely disappear...' Sound haiku talk!

> the old carp's
> red-cornered eyes—
> cherry petals falling

Mutsuo Takahashi
(*Haiku: The poetic key to Japan*, Mutsuo Takahasi, Hakudo Inoue, Kazuya Takaoka, PIE Books, Tokyo, 2003)

Eye-deology ... Haiku teaches us a path of deepening serenity. It is not an anaesthetic. Disappearing is not running away. With no full stop at the end, the haiku experience trails off into infinity. Its taste lingers long after we have returned to so-called normal consciousness.

All we have to do, then, is to see – it's an eye-deology! 'If thine eye is clear...' We do not have to know anything:

> Primavera
> Spring has come now
> No one knows how

Antonio Machado

134

the orchard path
disappearing
into blossom haze

Patricia Neubauer
(Four Seasons)

—~~~—

A time for every purpose ... In today's world there is an unremitting
bombardment of sexual imagery, much of it unsolicited. In haiku and
senryu we see sex as a normal healthy activity – but not something that is
meant to be incessant:

deep in the ground
male and female organs too
are hibernating

Kakujirō

The profound wisdom of haiku is rooted in the rhythms, colours, sounds,
sights, odours and moods of seasonal activity, singly and together. A time
for every purpose under heaven. How swiftly haiku penetrates to the
manifold mystery of time:

snow again—
how much my son's footprint
have grown

Izumi Kaneko
(International Haiku Magazine 'Troubadour', Ginyu, No. 21, 2004)

—~~~—

Haiku can teach us a joyous – not a gloomily fatalistic – acceptance of the
world as it is. Reading and writing haiku brings us ever closer to what a
spring morning is, or an autumn evening, until we disappear into its mystery
and become one with the rain, the sunshine, experiencing the nature of
morningness or nightness fully in themselves, with our invisible
participation. For a split second, the world can belong to a *hototogiso*, a
little mountain cuckoo:

135

> making an echo
> a hototogiso
> sings as it pleases

Hisajo

It is as it is. It might also be more than it is. There's a Japanese saying: 'The bird that cries *korokoro* in the mountain rice-field I know to be a *hototogiso* – yet it may have been my father, it may have been my mother.'

Ari no mama, things as they are, no embellishments, no gilding of the lily, this is found in the folk-literature of all lands:

> if nothing touches
> the palm-leaves
> they do not rustle

African proverb

Shakespeare emphasises in *King John* what the haikuist instinctively knows:

> To gild refinéd gold, to paint the lily,
> To throw a perfume on the violet,
> To smooth the ice, or add another hue
> Unto the rainbow, or with taper light
> To seek the beauteous eye of heaven to garnish,
> Is wasteful and ridiculous excess...

Shakespeare

Issa's work, like that of all great haikuists, is imbued with *ari no mama:*

> the snail
> goes to sleep and wakes up
> just as he is

Issa
(*A Haiku Menagerie*)

In things as they are we find real insight, real contentment and haiku is one of the most powerful tools available to all of us towards this end, which is not an end but an experience of no-beginning, no-end:

> evening hailstones
> lashing the branches —
> their whiteness

Suju Takano

Things as they are. Just so! No striving. Becoming the invisible haiku witness, the whiteness, the silent participant. **Wallace Stevens** in *Adagia* declares, 'The poet is the priest of the invisible.'

> In growing dark
> only the sound falls:
> dry magnolia leaf

Anna Holley
(*Four Seasons*)

Alive alive-o!

Enlightenment is any experience
    of expanding our consciousness
    beyond its present limits.
    We could also say that perfect enlightenment
    is realizing that we have no limits at all,
    and that the entire universe is
    alive . . .

Thaddeus Golas
(*Lazy Man's Guide to Enlightenment,* 1972)

—⁓—

Is it safe to disappear? From minute to minute we change. The entity we call the (inflated) self, what exactly was it some minutes ago, some years ago? The same? Surely not!

The real Self is unchanging. Some people who experiment with advanced techniques of meditation   without the necessary physiological and neurological stability needed for the job, or with an inadequate intellectual understanding of the mechanics of consciousness – such people can experience traumatic personality disorders. Stuff from the past can surface and unhinge us. Haiku, on the other hand, is a safe technique. Please refer to our title – the *gentle* art of disappearing. The haikuist momentarily identifies with the phenomena perceived in the haiku moment – "so close an identification with the object that the unstable mentalizing self disappears". (Introduction, *The Penguin Book of Zen Poetry*, ed. Lucien Stryk).

For the haikuist who has too many thoughts, some form of physical work is recommended – walking, doing some chores with the hands. This is why we see so many orders of monks engaged in physical work in the fields. It's important to achieve a balance.

One may also favour foods and beverages that tend to cool rather than excite the physiology. *Brahmi* is an Ayurvedic herb which can increase alertness and strengthen the central nervous system and *Mentat* is a powerful Ayurvedic combination of herbs which pacifies the overactive mind. Green tea is also good for calming and clarity.

There are also certain types of music which may be good for the brain, traditional Irish music, traditional percussion from Bali (gamelan), classical Baroque, classical Indian music. **Mozart** has a calming and elevating effect on many people. So, calm alertness is the key to haiku – and to so much else in life.

Francis Story (*Dimensions of Buddhist Thought*, Buddhist Publication Society, Kandy, Sri Lanka 1976) was not talking about haiku, but we may draw upon his insights for our purposes here: 'Having risen from that Absorption, the mind will be calm and concentrated, and being no longer disturbed by desires of the more active kind, it becomes able to examine the factors of experience with detachment, and so enjoys a new clarity of perception. It is as though the rippled surface of a pool were to become smooth and still; when that happens two things follow: the surface reflects external things more accurately, and at the same time it becomes possible to see through the surface to the depths below...'

Seen in the context of haiku, these words have a universal significance and application: the clarity that arises from absorption in the haiku moment can be expressed in the universal language of haiku, for all to share and enjoy.

Differences between us, historical and current, these differences melt down in the haiku crucible. Absorption, it could be said, is merely the first step towards an ever-deepening awareness of the value of the haiku experience. Many do not get as far as this first step and so their haiku never deepen. But one genuine haiku moment definitely leads to another, triggering off an evolutionary mechanism in consciousness, something which is latently present in all of us, uncreated and indestructible. This evolutionary mechanism drew you to this book in the first place!

An awakening ... Haiku is an awakening into this world, our birthplace. A living world:

> wind in the pines
> giving the emptiness
> a sound

Adele Kenny
(*Migrating Geese*, Muse-Pie Press, 1987)

> matter of great urgency
> a nut rolls away
> alive

Soen Nakagawa

—⁓—

Re-invent haiku? Re-invent the wheel! There may be a double-take in this nut haiku. The nut appears to be moving as if on some urgent business; or its movement – without any intention – can be seen as very important in itself, in the sense that everything within our field of haiku awareness is of the highest significance. Some people would say only a nut could understand this strange haiku. It is too Japanese. "Too Zen, babe", they say.

Unfortunately, a certain arrogance has crept into the haiku world – and nothing could be more out of place in this or in any other world than arrogance; it is an arrogance that belittles tradition and that suggests we should be free of all the trappings and influences that have coalesced, over time – in ways we may never fathom – and that have made haiku what it is; therefore, this arrogance claims we can walk before we crawl!

> step by step
> a new-born lamb
> eternal spring

Soen Nakagawa

> the tiny nightingale
> stutters
> and starts again

Chiyo-ni

The School of Arrogance hopes for a Western-style haiku, a haiku independent of its origins. It says we can forget about Taoist poetry, classical *renku* (linked verse), Zen Buddhism with its Chinese and Indian antecedents, *koans* (mind-boggling riddles), Pure Land Buddhism, Shinto, animism, superstition, folklore, custom, the signs, portents, moods and rituals associated with seasonal themes and events, the life and work of individual haiku masters, the sound of the *shakuhachi* (the bamboo flute), the temple bell, the endless layers of cultural and literary reference, the whole gamut of commonplace and esoteric symbol and cosmology. As if the West could possibly live on its own!

We do not need a detailed, scholarly knowledge of everything listed above and there are paths of awareness that, historically, owe nothing to Zen, but the least we can do is absorb good haiku from original sources, accepting the inadequacy of translation.

Soen Nakagawa collected pebbles on his travels. He kept them in a bag. He liked to swing the bag on occasions:

> touching one another
> each becomes
> a pebble of the world
>
> **Soen Nakagawa**

This simple haiku should become the motto of the emerging world haiku movement.

—☽—

Be a nut ... If an anti-Zennist cannot see a nut, or contemplate a nut, or see eternity in a nut, he shrugs and blames it on the impenetrability or irrelevance of Zen; instead, should he not examine the mote in his own eye and understand the self-imposed limits on his perceptions?

Limited perception arises from struggling in the snare of duality, an inability to let go, to penetrate and interpenetrate, to flow and merge. Is there a way out of this predicament? Yes: in a word, disappear.

Zen is just another word. Why get worked up about it? It's foreign to you, you say? Look at the pebble. Is a pebble foreign to you? A nut? Be a nut. Vanish entirely into nut-ingness!

waking from a nap
dewy mountain
approaching

Modorijo

Do you think we disappear when we are asleep? No, it is when we awake
we disappear. Awakening to our true nature, our true home. The universe.
In which we must disappear if we are to be there.

Haiku is a great, eventful homecoming. The Swedes say that people
over fifty are strangers in their own land. True. So many changes occur in
the space of fifty years, changes in mores, eating and drinking, speech,
taste, doing business, the arts and sciences, the physical environment and so
on. There is a lot of alienation out there. Does not the earth appear,
sometimes, to be populated by millions of exiles, legions of the displaced?

my native place
whenever I turn to look
mountains smile

Shiki

Let's all go home! We have been wandering long enough. This planet, this
universe, this galaxy is our home. Near and far. And we share it with
thousands and thousands of other species whose home this was before we
tumbled on the scene.

Who do you think you are?

Cognition, higher consciousness, even perhaps conscience and a soul
are attributes we assign to ourselves in our desire for self-definition.
We suppose that we alone have a notion of transcendence – but, like
most of our claims to unique sagacity, this is a result of our inability to
communicate with other species. It is like dismissing as dumb the
people whose speech you cannot understand…

— **Felipe Fernández-Armesto** (*Civilizations*, Pan Books, 2000)

—⁓—

Difficult to disappear? It is difficult for us to disappear. Our shoes, our
wallet, our watch, clothes, car keys, credit cards and all the other
appurtenances that **Chief Tuiavii** was trying to imagine. How do we

141

unburden ourselves? Go on a streaking mission? No, you will be more visible than ever before.

Seifu-jo had to wait until everyone else had gone to bed before she could disappear:

> everyone asleep
> nothing will come
> between the moon and me
>
> **Seifu-jo**

—〰—

alone tonight
      with the tadpoles
      with the universe

Describing his enlightenment **Dōgen** summed it up as this: 'Body and mind dropped off!' Exactly as **Santōka** said. Of course, **Santōka** was addicted to rice wine. Did alcohol numb his sense of being in a body or cloud his mind? Not at all:

> Slightly tipsy;
> The leaves fall
> One by one

Santōka

(Mountain Tasting, Zen Haiku by Santoka Taneda, John Stevens, Weatherhill 1980)

———

The body. Ah, the body... How do you think of your body? It might be helpful to consider this, from **Francis Lucille**: 'Your body is in you. You are not in it.'

———

Permanence and impermanence ... Haiku is terrific when it comes to drilling the essential message of flux and *mujō*, impermanence:

> cuckoo call—
> a monk wrote haiku on a rock
> and journeyed on

Haritsu

———

There was a time when all peoples had this wisdom, when the sayings of the elders had poetry and weight. As **Crowfoot**, a Blackfoot warrior and noted orator, said: 'What is life? It is the flash of a firefly in the night. It is the breath of a buffalo in the wintertime. It is the little shadow which runs across the grass and loses itself in the sunset...' This is not some syncretic sleight of hand. Truly, there is no distinction whatsoever between the spirit of **Crowfoot** and the spirit of haiku master **Bashō**!

Scientifically and technologically we are in a position to "conquer" outer space, to "civilize" other planets. But what do we mean by civilization? What do we know? We've learned nothing.

We are forgetting what really matters. We continue to repeat the mistakes of previous generations and have not retained what those generations knew to be beautiful, good, healthy and wise. We cannot, we must not press forward anymore; we must not expand blindly with no concept of sustainability. We must, in fact, beat a retreat, savour once more the creative core of silence, the flow of silence, out of which the thousand things emerge anew.

There are thousands of ways to our senses. Haiku is one. A beautiful way. Haiku masters have shown us how. The path awaits you.

> its voice
>   stolen by the moonlight—
>   the white cat

Sayumi Kamakura

———

Head without a body … Think of ten or so of the twentieth century's greatest American writers and intellectuals. It is quite amazing how few of them make any reference at all to the literature and the wisdom of the First Nation peoples, as if the essence of this culture was somehow alien or totally irrecoverable.

America will never be at home with the world or with itself until it is at home, again, with what it has replaced. Intellectuality, that fails to embrace its indigenous shadowland is a head without a body. Haiku is body and head as one, disappearing in spirit.

May we quote **George Santayana** here? 'Progress, far from consisting in change, depends on retentiveness.' Haikuists, in particular, must delve into the invisible past to create nature-haiku of that intuitive connection with landscape and remembered landscape which came so readily to First Nation poets and minstrels.

This is not easy to do unless one first sacrifices one's false sense of ego, of self, of identity. Addressing the Class of 2003, **Susan Sontag,** Vassar College, said: 'Try to imagine at least once a day that you are not an American.' She could as easily have said, 'Try to imagine at least once a day that you are a Native American;' the native peoples, through the eyes of **John Muir**, 'walk softly and hurt the landscape hardly more than the birds and squirrels.'

———

145

Waxing and waning ... We must re-imagine our own humanity. So, what are you? Your body? Your name? Your mind? Your personality?

Swami Vivekananda cautions us: 'The body is not the Real Man; neither is the mind, for the mind waxes and wanes. It is the Spirit beyond which alone can live forever... Every particle in this body is continually changing; no one has the same body for many minutes together, and yet we think of it as the same body...' Will that make it easier for us to disappear? Disappearing... It's not easy, at first. Easier for birds:

> in bare branches
> the naked love
> of sparrows

> **Darko Plažanin**
> (*Sparrow*, 27-28, Croatia)

—*/\/\/*—

Resistance to disappearing ... The ego will resist. Of course it will. The bigger your ego, the greater the resistance. 'It is okay to have a big ego, but point it in the right direction. Point it at the stars and on the way it will fall away...' (*This Marvellous Ego* by **Michael Barnett**, Cosmic Energy Connections, 1999). Or beyond the stars:

> the last sounds of rain—
> the sickle moon rises into
> starless infinity

> **Jasminka Nadaskic Djordjevic**

In a very practical sense, the Finns knew how advantageous it was to be able to disappear. White-clad Finnish skiers resisted a superior military force by being able to disappear at will and outwit the visible ones.

—*/\/\/*—

Luminosity of being ... Yes, if the ego is not pointed at the stars, how difficult it is to disappear. What are we to do? Does the office disappear too? Our home? Our loved ones? The dog? The TV set? We seem to forget, most of the time, that we are 'luminous beings' (see *Tales of Power*, **Carlos Castaneda**).

Easier for clouds to move, to change, to disappear:

a low cloud
pushes the day
westwards

Dunja Pezelj
(*Sparrow*, 27-28, Croatia)

What magic is required to disappear? Haiku magic! Only by seeing can we disappear:

after the rain
a spider mends its net
with a rainbow

Nedeljka Lupis
(Sparrow, 27-28, Croatia)

Jasminka (above) isn't pushing the sickle moon, **Dunja** isn't shoving the cloud, **Nedeljka** is not patching up the web. All over the world, happily, thousands of haikuists are appearing. Here, however, we are more interested in their vanishing acts. As former editor-in-chief of *The Heron's Nest*, **Christopher Herold**, reminds us: 'Haiku practice has the capacity to reunite us with things from which we've set ourselves apart through SELF consciousness.'

winter galaxy
my aged body
slumbers deeply

Sonoko Nakamura

Chanting to disappear ... The self can disappear in such activities and performances as martial arts, meditation, prayer, bhakti poetry, haiku and chanting. For **Issa** and **Chiyo**, Pure Land Buddhism offered endless opportunities which might go unnoticed by the faithless:

even the butterfly—
voiceless
Buddhist service

Chiyo-ni

could they be hymns?
frogs are chanting
in the temple well

Kansetsu
(*A Haiku Menagerie*)

coo-cooing to itself
the pigeon . . .
until it has no self

GR

—·ɯɯ·—

This floating world ... Things change, things return, things go away, things vanish in this floating world as in this very clever take by **Bōsai** on **Bashō**'s famous *furuike ya*:

an old pond—
after jumping in,
no frog

Bōsai
(*A Haiku Menagerie*)

Seeing nothing: this is also something.

jumping back in the pond
what only yesterday
was a tadpole

GR

short summer night
floating among rushes
bubbles from a crab

Buson

—·ɯɯ·—

Universal voice ... While it is generally considered that **Bashō** and **Buson** were more sophisticated than that country bumpkin, **Issa**, it can be argued that **Issa** is not only the most engagingly human of all haiku masters but that his wisdom, ultimately, is the purest:

> no need to wail—
> wherever you fly, wild geese,
> it's the same floating world
>
> **Issa**

> goose, wild goose!
> when did your journey
> begin!
>
> **Issa**

The richness of his wisdom derives from a powerful combination of his extraordinary unalloyed devotion to the Buddha, absorption of peasant lore, his striking humility, his humour, his immense compassion and fortitude in the face of the vicissitudes of life; these qualities, and more, are all reflected in the variety of his prolific output. Yes, **Bashō** is frequently more mysterious:

> when the eyes
> of the hawk darken
> the quail calls
>
> **Bashō**

But **Issa**, too, is capable of mystery, of plumbing the very origins of his being, his faith, his world:

> from the nostril
> of the Great Buddha comes
> a swallow
>
> **Issa**
> (*A Haiku Menagerie*)

It is inexplicable that such an immortal is excluded from so many major anthologies of world poetry. Hopefully, **David G. Lanoue**'s ongoing translations of **Issa** on the internet will help to remove **Issa** from the footnotes of world literature and place him, finally, among the pantheon. Of course, when this happens **Issa**'s first reaction will be to compose a haiku:

> pantheon . . .
> winter loneliness
> no fleas

GR

Vanishing and reappearing, growing old with haiku, with a child's pure heart, **Issa** is constantly in sacramental union with everything that comes to his hut and everything that leaves it:

> seeing that I'm old
> even the mosquito whispers
> closer to my ear

Issa
(*Haiku People*)

—*w*—

The Creator gathered all of creation together
and spoke these words:
'I want to hide something from the humans – until they are ready for it.
It is this: the realization that they create their own reality!'
The Eagle said: 'Give it to me. I will take it to the Moon.'
The Creator said: 'No, one day they will go there and find it.'
The Salmon said: 'I will hide it on the floor of the Ocean.'
'No,' said the Creator. 'They will go there too.'
The Buffalo spoke: 'I will bury it on the Great Plains.'
The Creator said: 'They will cut into the skin of the Earth and find it.'
Grandmother Mole, who lives in the breast of Mother Earth, and who
has no physical eyes but sees with spiritual eyes, said:
'Put it inside them.'
The Creator said: 'It is done.'

(*Sioux Legend*)

Live and let live ... When we lose sympathetic contact with nature, one species after the other – unless we can eat it – becomes an annoyance, an irrelevance. Pests! This attitude eventually extends to members of our own species whose attractiveness or usefulness may become questionable to us. And then it begins all over again, man's inhumanity to man. Haiku can break this vicious circle in numerous ways. **Issa** can teach us how to live and let live... May his haiku proliferate in the remaining languages of the earth.

—⁓—

Infinite patience ... If haiku is a way of interpenetrating with the visible signs of the universe's constant regeneration, it does so by teaching us infinite patience:

> a white chrysanthemum—
> however much I look
> no speck of dust

Bashō

We gaze, intently, emptily, until the flower reveals its immaculate whiteness. The joy of haiku is this: contemplation and meditation, usually seen as distinct practices, become one in an electric stillness. This is one of haiku's great gifts to the world, to you. If you are ready to receive these gifts, they will come, unbidden:

> ill in bed
> the cat brings me
> a scent from the garden

Stephen Toft
(*Blithe Spirit*, Vol. 12, No. 2, Sept. 2002)

A fresh scent from outside becomes stronger than the whiff of medicines or the stale odour of illness – the living world becomes more significant than our condition. What is often expressed loftily or in abstract terms in the world's religious and mystic traditions becomes concretized or crystallized in haiku.

In *Songs of the Ultimate* (*Hymns from Shankaracharya and Abhinavagupta,* collected and edited by Éric Baret, Absent Crocodile Publication, Athens, 1994) we read:

Wherever you find yourself, stay.
Go neither towards the outside nor the inside.
Let the infinite variations of becoming be cast aside
by the glowing of Consciousness alone . . .

—⁓—

Wisdom tradition ... Certainly we should be open to all wisdom traditions; they are part of mankind's inheritance. But does not the best of haiku also belong to a wisdom tradition, a tradition of silent witnessing with the whole heart and all of the senses and, furthermore, one that is essentially inclusive, non-elitist, open to all, and within everyone's compass and capability?

> scraping a parsnip
>   still not as white
>   as Bashō's chrysanthemum

GR

> my eyes, having seen all,
>   came back to
>   the white chrysanthemums

Issho

> edge of town
> a gypsy's horse
> drinks winter rain

Matt Morden
(*Snapshots #7*, 2000)

Cleaning the slate ... The haiku moment presents us with a *tabula rasa* each and every time. To clean a parsnip is neither pleasant nor unpleasant. Just something to be done. Looking at a chrysanthemum. No big deal. The gypsy's horse takes a drink. Has to be done. As simple as that.

Marcus Aurelius, a Roman emperor (121 –180), had a way with words: 'If you are pained by external things, it is not they that disturb you, but your own judgement of them. And it is in your power to wipe out that judgement now.' A wise man by all accounts, and there is much in his twelve books of *Meditations* that reminds one of **Confucius**; both advocates of tranquillity still have a certain relevance today, in our unquiet world.

Looking around us, examining various national and international scenarios, can we say, hand on heart, that our rulers are wise and that their utterances promote tranquillity among their own people and among nations? Why have rulers anyway? Why should they rule us? Should they not simply serve us in the spirit of wisdom and the brotherhood of mankind?

Of course, **Aurelius** was caught up in wars, also, mostly of a defensive nature. And, admittedly, he gave Christians a hard time. But his domestic policy was enlightened and his care for the poor extended to selling his own possessions in order to help victims of hunger and plague.

Where are the political and religious leaders to emulate such action today? Don't you wish that some of our leaders might just disappear for a while?!

> slave cemetery
> i scrape the moss to find
> no name
>
> **William M. Ramsey**
> (*This Wine*, 2002)

> harvest moon
> my ashes
> still wrapped in flesh
>
> **William M. Ramsey**
> (*ibid.*)

a winter moon
      came out to play
           alone

GR

Recite Aloud

Thinking

Now that all thoughts have subsided
off I go, deep into the woods,
and pick me
a handful of shepherd's purse.
Just like the stream
meandering through mossy crevices
I, too, hushed,
become utterly clear

Ryokan

Haiku and invisibility … Since each pure haiku moment is a cleansing of the heart and mind – a diamond-point of concentrated illumination, a link-up with the unsullied – it can be said that the haikuist comes to be in perfect touch with her/ his own inherent invisibility and perfection. And this invisibility becomes more and more of a reality as haiku moments become richer, deeper and more refined.

St. Augustine of Hippo says: 'Some men of great gifts, and very learned in the Holy Scriptures, who have, when an opportunity presented itself, done much by their writings to benefit the Church and promote the instruction of believers, have said that the invisible God is seen in an invisible manner, that is, by that nature which in us also is invisible, namely, a pure mind or heart.'

Becoming dew … Why suffer like the Prince of Denmark – 'Oh that this too, too solid flesh would melt, thaw and resolve itself into a dew…' It is purity of mind, a purity of heart which allows us to recognise the dew and share in its nature:

dance, from one blade of grass
to another—
pearls of dew!

Ransetsu

Shakespeare's greatness as a tragedian rests largely on his supreme ability to depict the tragic consequences of the dualistic mind. Peace and lack of peace are constant themes:

> Pour the sweet milk of concord into hell,
> Uproar the universal peace, confound
> All unity on earth
>
> (*Macbeth*)

This contrasts with the opposite mood:

> And this our life, exempt from public haunt,
> Finds tongues in trees, books in the running brooks,
> Sermons in stones, and good in everything . . .
>
> (*As You Like It*)

He is often concerned with the poisoned mind, the loss of wisdom – as when Othello moans, 'Farewell the tranquil mind!'

The haiku path, on the other hand, is one of conflict resolution. How can Oneness be in conflict? The great master **Dōgen** puts it like this: 'When the opposites arise, the Buddha mind is lost.'

Shakespeare sees the problem clearly:

> Sigh no more, ladies, sigh no more,
> Men were deceivers ever;
> One foot in sea, and one on shore,
> To one thing constant never.
>
> (*Much Ado About Nothing*)

Of course, if he only dwelt in the realm of duality, physicality and visibility, **Shakespeare** would not be the great playwright that he is. No – the invisible world, the transcendental world – as must be – finds its place in his work; on Cleopatra's lips, arranged here in 17 syllables:

> Give me my robe
> Put on my crown
> I have immortal longings in me

—ᴧᴧ—

Invisible heart of the world ... Haiku reconnects us with the invisible, beating heart of the world. The Sami have a beautiful legend, as pure as the snow that surrounds them. The creator-god took the living, trembling heart out of a young reindeer and buried it deep in the centre of the earth. In times of tribulation, the Sami nomads have only to put an ear to the ground and listen and know that all will be well – the heart still beats.

Haiku is a way of listening just as much as seeing:

> does the woodpecker
> stop and listen, too?
> evening temple drum
>
> **Issa**

Once we are open, who knows what guides may appear:

> the moon
> has found it for me
> a mountain path
>
> **Michael McClintock**

> without a voice
> the heron would disappear—
> morning snow
>
> **Chiyo-ni**

Chiyo-ni became a nun in 1775. Why? To flow! To vanish, 'to teach my heart to be like the clear water which flows night and day!'

réalta
crann
is an tnúthán eatarthu

a star
a tree
and the longing in between

Mahavir vanishes … One can take it that **Aurelius** was lavish without giving every blessed thing away. The great Indian saint **Mahavir** went one step further than our Roman friend. He gave all his princely wealth away in one grand gesture, leaving himself with nothing but the cloak on his back. In his haste to flee the world, a thorny bush snagged his cloak, tearing half of it away. **Mahavir** now had only half of a cloak. Along comes a hobbling beggar. He had heard that **Mahavir** was giving away all of his earthly goods. Had he missed the event? Was he too late? **Mahavir** gave the poor beggar all he possessed – the remaining half of his cloak – and vanished, naked, into the forest. Free at last!

In pure, selfless haiku moments, we become the vanishing **Mahavir**. There is nothing we can take with us on this journey of light.

———

Santōka, the beggar monk, was in his ramshackle abode when a dog appeared. It had a rice-biscuit in its mouth. Much appreciated as his begging bowl was rarely full. He split the biscuit with the dog! That wasn't enough. A hungry cat appeared. He split it again:

> Autumn night—
>> got it from the dog
>>> gave it to the cat

Santōka

———

A delicate concatenation … Many haiku double their effect by introducing subtle counter-images or companion-images and one never ceases to wonder, even after repeated readings, at all that's going on, all that's being suggested, within this little form:

> the sea darkens
>> the voice of the duck
>>> faintly white

Bashō

> the falling leaves
>> fall and pile up; the rain
>>> beats on the rain

Gyôdai

It is, of course, an event – one event – that is described in a haiku but in it we discover layers of experience, an accumulation of happenings, a delicate concatenation of related, universal, timeless events. Haiku moments are in the eternal now. **Silesius**, as we have said before, intuits this valuable insight:

> Time is eternity, eternity is time,
> If you wish, you can make them rhyme

> **Angelus Silesius**

—*⁄∿⁄*—

Alertness in the One ... Have you noticed how often rain has occurred in the sample haiku given so far? And will you notice the word 'rain' the next time it occurs?

It is going to occur again fairly soon. Stay alert! And even if it doesn't occur again, stay alert anyway. (Or take another timely break NOW)

In the **Gyôdai** haiku (above) we have noticed leaves upon leaves and rain on rain. Are these separate entities or are they one? If they were separate entities it would be impossible to disappear into one element and not into the other. One disappears into the whole. One cannot disappear into a fraction because fractions do not really exist. This is the important point we find in **Shunryu Suzuki**'s enlightened text, *Zen Mind, Beginner's Mind* (Weatherhill, 1970): 'Each existence depends on something else. Strictly speaking, there are no separate individual existences. There are just many names for one existence.'

> charcoal
> drawing the tree
> it was

> **Sandra Fuhringer**
> (*The Tree it Was*, King's Road Press, 2002)

Everything is everything else – as is touchingly revealed in an anonymous poem collected in India in the 1st. century A.D. by **King Hala**:

Buck and Doe

There's a clearing in the forest
　　where a lone buck stands
　　　　desire is filling the eyes of a doe

The hunter in the trees
　　it's his own girl he sees
　　　　and drops the bow

King Hala

―᪲᪲᪲―

Unexpected showers ... Enjoy them! Rain, hail, sleet, or snow. The noise.
The silence. Penetrating to the essence:

　　　snow

　　　　　falling on snow—

　　　　　　　silence

Santōka

―᪲᪲᪲―

Penetrating the void ...

　　　　　winter wind
　　　　　　from where to where?
　　　　　　leafless trees

Chiyo-ni

Mediatate on This

The Saviour said, All nature, all formations,
all creatures exist in and with one another, and
they will be resolved again into their own roots.

The Gospel of Mary Magdalene

―᪲᪲᪲―

Sudden illumination ...

> flash of lightning!
>> legs of a spider
>>> scurrying up a wall

> **Kichō**

That lightning flash was no mere natural phenomenon; it was **Kichō**'s sudden illumination. The spider's legs, it has often been noticed, can be seen as a miniature pictogram of forked lightning scrawled on the sky. They are, in a way, the same. Inside is outside. Outside is inside. They are one. And **Kichō**, too, is at one with the one. Where else could he be? Outside? Inside? He is at one with the one – a feat impossible without disappearing in a flash.

In truth, every moment is vanishing, every sound is dying, and everything is being reborn. Catch these dying sounds while you can – disappear into them:

> three times they call
>> and then . . . no more . . .
>>> deer in rain

> **Buson**

Vanishing, dying – yes; and yet there's a palpable sense of eternity in **Buson**'s brief lines. The ever-curious mind may, in time, wonder what may have happened before, or after, but for one glorious, unrepeatable moment we hear a snatch of the unfinished symphony of life, its faint echo.

Cameron Burgess could well have been writing about haiku in the following: 'In truth, there is no teaching, there is no 'way' to be or not to be, to do or not to do. In truth, there is only the ever-deepening knowing that it is not the seer, the seen or the seeing that matters, but the place in which all three rest, the awareness of all three. This is who you are...' And this 'ever-deepening knowing' comes to all dedicated haikuists.

It can come in a flash as *kensho*, an opening, or as *satori*, enlightenment. These 'openings' are not deliberate, pre-meditated actions, such as uncorking a bottle of wine. They come to all who learn and perfect the art, they come as unexpected showers:

> the skylark:
> > its voice alone fell
> > leaving nothing behind

Ampu

(R. H. Blyth)

—⋙—

Everything is coming and going in this world of dew, including our own manifestations and disappearances. We can disappear at will when our vision penetrates and interpenetrates an event until all clutter dissolves. This from a book called *Mit weinig woorden*, (With a few words), published in Flanders in 1997:

> the grey sea
> darkens in the evening
> the void grows

Ferre Denis
(Willy Cuvelier & Ferre Denis)

The haikuist knows how to slip into that void. He does it all the time. And the haikuist who doesn't know how to slip into that void is simply practising the form and had better start again *ab initio*.

> coming from fog
> > the bird flies through fog
> > fading into fog

Dimitar Stefanov

—⋙—

Revolutionary symphony... The veil of Maya, illusion, is as impenetrable in Bulgaria as it is in Flanders or as it is in the Himalayas but haiku consciousness rends that veil, momentarily. No rituals are needed. We need not sit impassively like ascetic yogis until, as **Kabir** says, our matted locks make us look like goats. Meditative readings of the Haiku Masters is an apprenticeship in itself and initiates responsive readers to recognise and experience haiku moments in their ordinary, everyday lives. The result will be the birth of a revolutionary symphony.

William Henry Channing could have been talking about the haiku path when he said:

'To live content with small means; to seek elegance rather than luxury, and refinement rather than fashion; to be worthy, not respectable, and wealthy, not rich; to listen to stars and birds, babes and sages with open heart; to study hard; to think quietly, act frankly, talk gently, await occasions, hurry never, in a word, to let the spiritual, unbidden and unconscious grow up through the common – this is my symphony.'

It is much more than a symphony. It is a revolution! Engagement with haiku is a revolutionary act. And – so far – it's legal! 'Seeking elegance rather than luxury' is a revolutionary statement in our grasping, selfish world; 'to listen to stars and birds' competes with the frivolity of mass media, the noisy might of corporate television and radio, the strident, gossipy entertainment industry; 'to be content with small means' flies in the face of rampant consumerism.

Haiku is a revolutionary symphony that can save the world from its own vapidity, selfishness, greed, cruelty … from all of its gross excesses. To disappear, in haiku, is the most revolutionary act of all! It is truly a mark of our daring, our freedom:

> snow flurrying . . .
> the deer look back, one by one
> before they vanish

> **Tom Clausen**
> (*Standing Here*, self-published 1998)

Where have all the young men gone?

> Marching together
> On the ground
> They will never step on again

> **Santōka**
> (*John Stevens*)

Gently fading …

october dawn
a pheasant fades
into the cotton field

Darrel Byrd
(World Haiku Association web site)

cry of the hawk
long after
it has disappeared

Kat Avila
(*ibid.*)

———

Apocalyptic vision … On receiving the Börne Prize, world-acclaimed literary critic and philosopher, **George Steiner**, reminded us that we are guests on this earth. We should behave courteously, graciously. His speech of thanks had an apocalyptic warning: 'Tons of rubbish, of poisonous filth, lie on Mount Everest. Seas are dying. Innumerable plants and animal species are being destroyed…' **Steiner** makes us ask ourselves, what kind of guests are we at all?

We should listen to that Psalm which, indeed, insists that we are no more than mere guests on this earth. The composer **Schütz** put some very beautiful music to **Luther**'s translation of that Psalm: '*Ich bin ein Gast auf Erden…*'

Back to **Steiner** now, his diagnosis, his prognosis: 'The guest has become a technologically intoxicated, blind vandal. He systematically wrecks the hostelry which had welcomed him…' Who could disagree? But, how is our planet going to recover? **Steiner**'s view is bleak: 'The environment will only recover after the self-destruction of a humanity made crazy by money mania. Only if we vanish does our planet have a chance…' (Quoted in *Kulturchronik* No. 2, 2003).

———

A peaceful vanishing … We concur with **Steiner**'s prognosis, in a way. After all, no less an authority on life forms on earth than **Jacques Cousteau** says the same thing, if we are not willing to turn away from greed 'we will disappear from the face of the globe, to be replaced by the insect.'

But we see it differently from **Steiner** and **Cousteau**. Vanish, disappear, yes, but not in a suicidal holocaust, not in violence, not in fire and brimstone. We can all learn to disappear now, to walk lightly on this earth, to treasure the world and hold it in awe:

> a pheasant's tail
> very gently brushes
> the violets

Shushiki
(*A Haiku Menagerie*, Stephen Addiss with Fumiko & Akira Yamamoto (Weatherhill, 1992)

The haikuist's disappearance allows him a companionableness with the rest of nature, an unthreatening, invisible, compassionate, healing presence:

> morning chill
> one mushroom
> shelters another

Mark Brooks

And the return from these almost shamanistic voyages can also be described:

> the geese fly off . . .
> and now it comes to me
> that I am still here

H. F. Noyes
(*Parnassus Literary Journal*, Fall 1988)

—◦◦◦—

In the haiku moment interpenetration occurs with the visible and the invisible, the near and the far, the temporal and the eternal:

> summer evening
> light that touched the moon
> touching me

Michael Ketchek
(*Acorn*, No. 4, 2000)

166

scarecrow
still measuring
the vast summer sky

Ty Hadman
(*The Heron's Nest*, 2001)

By being invisible, we hear better:

listen!
the skins of wild damsons
darkening in the rain

Caroline Gourlay
(*Reading All Night*, Hub Haiku Series, 2000)

—*ᴠᴠ*—

There it is again ... The rain! We warned you it was coming. Remember? Were you alert to it? There might be another shower on the way, so watch out.

An other-world aura surrounds the above haiku. If fairies and other ethereal beings didn't exist, we would have to invent them! It is our fairy-like ability to be invisible, to move as the wind shifteth, this is what allows us extraordinary moments of numinous presence and an awareness of the living presence of other things, animate and seemingly inanimate:

winter night.
the mannequin in the shop window
stares at my jumper

Nikola Madzhirov
(*Ginyu*, No. 20, 20/10/2003)

Our hearing improves dramatically with haiku!

deep in the shadows
of this forgotten temple
swallow chicks cry

Suezan Aikins
(*Four Seasons)*

167

Ich hőre sogar die Laute der Stille—
Zentempelgarten

I can even hear
the sound of quietness—
Zen garden

Gabi Greve
(Simply Haiku, 2006)

East and West

When the ancient man composed a poem, he felt that spiritual Power
spoke through him. In Greece the poet let the Muse speak through him
to his fellowmen. This consciousness was a heritage of the ancient
Orient. With the passage of the spiritual life toward the West, poetry
became more and more the manifestation of man himself. In the ancient
Orient, the spiritual Powers sang through man to men. The cosmic
word resounded from the gods down to man. In the West, it has become
the human word. It must find the way upward to the spiritual powers.
Man must learn to create poetry in such a way that the Spirit may listen
to him. The West must mould a language suited to the Spirit. Then the
East will say: "The divine Word, which once streamed for us from
heaven to earth, finds its way back from the hearts of men into the
spiritual world…"

— **Rudolf Steiner** (West-East Aphorisms)

Trust: the haiku way … By trusting in the haiku moment, you open
yourself up to the possibility of radical renewal and you will see that by
disappearing, you have not lost anything. You have gained. You have
gained the most important thing there is in life:

> Suddenly one day everything is empty like space
> That has no inside or outside, no bottom or top,
> And you are aware of one principle
> Pervading all the ten thousand things.
> You know then that your heart
> Is so vast that it can never be measured.

Daikaku

tú féin a lomadh
bheith leat féin, gan mhaisiú . . .
gaotha an fhómhair

tae staun nakit
be alane, hamelt . . .
hairst wunds

(John McDonald)

to bare oneself
be alone, unadorned . . .
autumn winds

Immeasurable heart ... When the haikuist experiences dissolving in the haiku moment, he learns that his heart 'is so vast that it can never be measured'. Then all things, near and far, fall into the compass of fearless compassion and wonder. It is not that his heart has expanded overnight, or in an instant. It is a dawning, an awareness of a hidden potential, which haiku awakens.

Haiku allows us to breathe, once freed of the fetters that cramp and limit our consciousness. Hitherto meaningless chores suddenly become rituals of surprise, beauty, awe and reverence. Every true haiku you read, every true haiku you write will sustain this insight and reflect it.

sweeping
and then not sweeping
the fallen leaves

Taigi
(*A Haiku Garden*, Addiss et al)

—◊◊◊—

When **Yeats** said 'I'm looking for the face I had before the world was made' he was talking about that state of egolessness which we once all knew. **Sogyal Rinpoche** says: 'It is important to remember always that the principle of egolessness does not mean that there was an ego in the first place – and the Buddhists did away with it! On the contrary, it means there was never any ego at all to begin with. To realize that is called 'egolessness'.

It is this 'egolessness' which affords **Taigi** such pleasure in sweeping up the leaves and in not sweeping them, investing action and inaction with dignity and meaning beyond words.

—◊◊◊—

Disappearance: will you recognise it? When you have genuine haiku moments, the evidence of your disappearance will appear in your haiku. Simple as that. Every haiku arising from a genuine haiku moment is not so much a learning as a de-learning, an unlearning, a return to the state described above by **Sogyal Rinpoche**.

young buck
about to mate
mountain rain

Issa

> stiffening the mushroom
> on the stump . . .
> winter rain

> **Issa**
> *(David G. Lanoue)*

> first winter rain—
> the world drowns
> in haiku

> **Issa**
> *(David G. Lanoue)*

Did the rain catch you out, or were you expecting it? We said it would rain again. It always does. Especially when we're not expecting it. Things just slip up on us, appear and disappear:

> summer rains—
> secretly one evening
> moon in the pines

> **Ryōta**
> *(A Haiku Garden)*

Only one who had entered the secret of secrets and disappeared could see such a thing. Ah, how he must have inspired and delighted his 3,000 haiku students!

―✍―

Haiku and the exemplary being ... Pure haiku stands out as something entirely at odds with the artistic trends of the past one hundred years or so. As **Anna Bonshek** (*ibid.*) points out: 'In this age of consumerism, the love of art is self-love in disguise ... today's artist can no longer be taken as an exemplary human being since his art, which is more an expression of his own personal concerns than that of human universals, is essentially narcissistic...' Truly, the last thing on such an artist's mind is to disappear! A self-centred haikuist (a contradiction in terms, surely) contributes not a droplet to the pool of awakened consciousness.

―✍―

Gentle art of disappearing … We have already established (or opined) that the true haiku moment is a sacred moment. We could have used many near-synonyms instead of 'disappearing', such as 'melting away' in the haiku moment. The distinguished philosopher **Nishida** uses 'merging': 'As long as we set up a subjective self in opposition to the objective world and try to unify that world by means of it, then no matter how great this self becomes, the unity will remain inescapably relative. An absolute unity is only gained by discarding the subjective unity and merging with an objective unity.' (*An Enquiry into the Good,* Trans. Masao Abe & Christopher Ives, Yale University Press, 1990).

Merging, vanishing, melting away, disappearing … Listen to the inspired words of **Jan van Ruysbroeck**: 'Spiritual inebriation is this; that a man receives more sensible joy and sweetness than his heart can either contain or desire. Spiritual inebriation brings forth many strange gestures in men. It makes some sing and praise God because of their fullness of joy, and some weep with great tears because of their sweetness of heart. It makes one restless in all his limbs, so that he must run and jump and dance; and so excites another that he must gesticulate and clap his hands. Another cries out with a loud voice, and so shows forth the plenitude he feels within; another must be silent and melt away…' Beautiful words, worth savouring. They were not intended to endorse haiku, of course not. Nor did **Angelus Silesius** favour animism, pantheism or the like … had he been told about Zen or Shinto he might well have recoiled in horror, at first. To be quoted liberally in the same book alongside such culturally disparate characters as **Ikkyu** and **Crowfoot** would appear to him as some monstrous abomination more than likely. And yet, the true haikuist (whether a religious believer or not) can relate to the couplets of the so-called cherubinical wanderer in ways that he may never have suspected:

> In Spirit senses are One and the same. True.
> Who sees God, tastes, feels, smells and hears Him too

Angelus Silesius

Ruysbroeck speaks of 'sweetness of heart'. Can there be a 'melting away' without this precious virtue? True haiku cultivates sweetness of heart. Sweetness of heart! It is a concept which doesn't have much coinage today. No one can read a few hundred of the 20,000 or so haiku by **Issa** without experiencing and absorbing his charming sensitivity and sweetness of heart.

When the heart learns to live with this sensitivity, it discovers that each day, any time of the year, reveals a beauty all of its own:

> autumn coming to an end
> frogs beginning
> to settle underground

Shogetsu

A hitherto invisible aura manifests itself:

> a snail is crawling
> in a glimmer of light
> entirely its own

Chiyoda Kuzuhiko
(Four Seasons)

Luminosity enters our world:

> the morning sun
> brightly
> rising above frosty woods

Dakotsu

> howl of a coyote—
> red cactus flowers open
> to the morning sun

Roberta Stewart
(*Four Seasons*)

In your own way,
however small, paint.

In your own way,
however small, make a haiku.

In your own way, however small,
sing a song, dance a little.

Celebrate and you will find that
the next moment brings more silence.

Osho

(*Yoga, the Alpha and the Omega, Vol. IV*)

D
O

I
T

Nights come alive as well as mornings …

> is it the night
>   or trees
>   that creep through the woods?

> > > **Seán Mac Mathúna**

morning snow—
>   where to throw away
>   the tea leaves?

> > **Chiyo-ni**

—∿∿—

Indoors as well as outdoors …

> all silent—
>   host, guest
>   white chrysanthemum

> > > **Ryōta**
> > > *(Seán Mac Mathúna)*

There is a pleasurable eeriness in the **Mac Mathúna** and in the **Ryōta** haiku, a certain unexpectedness. Their originality forces us to think, or react, originally with, as it were, a beginner's mind.

—∿∿—

Inner sanctum … The haikuist can disappear into the flesh, taste, shape, odour and colour of an apple where most mainstream poets are left behind, maintaining a visibility, a longing, outside of the event.

George Meredith saw a girl in an orchard. She bites into an apple and turns to look at him:

> Her twinkle between frank and shy
> My thirst to bite where she had bit . . .

> > **George Meredith**

175

This is beautiful, of course, but it is only on the verge of disappearance. It is still, at least, one foot in the world of duality and desire. Pseudo-haiku – the bulk of haiku today – is similarly self-reflexive.

The ninth century poetess **Ono no Komachi** is also on the verge of the flow, that delicate moment in which disappearance might or might not happen:

> This body
> grown fragile, floating,
> a reed cut from its roots . . .
> if a stream would ask me
> to follow, I'd go, I think

Ono no Komachi
(*The Ink Dark Moon*, Vintage Books, 1990)

Pure haiku dissolves in its own immaculate spirit, in untainted essence. True haiku probes the nature of reality and our perception of it. In *The Glowing Moment* we referred to what such sages as **Papaji** and **Wei Wu Wei** teach: 'We do not seize Reality. Reality seizes us.' Haiku does this in bringing the full shock and brilliance of the visible and invisible realms to our senses. It makes sense of everything, penetrating into our inner sanctum and, simultaneously, reverberating throughout the cosmic ocean. In this haiku world, we come to our senses, the angelic side of our being and the animal side are awake, as one.

This quality is rarely found today in mainstream literature. We can see it, however, in much Inuit poetry:

spring fjord

I was out in my kayak
I was out at sea in it
I was paddling
very gently in the fjord Ammassivik
There was ice in the water
and on the water a petrel
turned his head this way that way
Didn't see me paddling
Suddenly nothing but his tail
Then nothing
He plunged but not for me:
Huge head upon the water
Great hairy seal

Giant head with giant eyes, moustache
All shining and dripping
And the seal came gently towards me
Why didn't I harpoon him?
Was I sorry for him?
Was it the day, the spring day, the seal
Playing in the sun
Like me?

Anonymous (Pomes Eskimo)
(Armand Schwerner, after Paul-Émil Victor, *Shaking the Pumpkin,*
Junction Press, 1999)

Such vision! Such clarity! Such oneness! There is wonderful humanity in
this poem as well. It sings the shining moment now, the senses and the heart
all terribly alive. But this vision, this seeing the new in everyday things in
all their colour, shape, texture and movement, this is rare in our lives today
and rarer still in contemporary poetry. We must look to haiku if we wish
such vividness, such freshness, such immediacy to permeate our lives.

—◦∧∧◦—

Disappearing – a trick? Disappearing is not some kind of a trick with
which to impress your friends. If it's tricks you're after, study **Houdini** not
haiku. No tricks. No ego.

Every culture has some myth or legend, some proverb or anecdote to
remind us of the dangers of ego. **Sinend** – who gives her name to the River
Shannon – approached the well of knowledge but the well rose up and
drowned her. Self-effacement is necessary to experience the true haiku
moment.

> white plum blossoms
> absorbing the colour
> of morning
>
> **Buson**

What is white? What is colour? The great wonder of haiku is that we come
to know that nothing is fixed. As soon as we become mysteriously familiar
with some moment of becoming, some numinous embodiment, it changes
into something else. As *we* change. That is why we speak here of the gentle
art of disappearing. Reality is so momentary that only a haiku can catch it.
Softly, softly catchee monkey…

You have to be invisible! Master-photographer **Henri Cartier-Bresson,** in a filmed interview, defined the key to his art as this: 'You have to be invisible!' Describing photography he says, 'It's a dance... Fully living in the instant!' This is similar to the flow of Tao mentioned in our opening pages. 'You don't take the photo. It's the photo that takes you,' he says. This, in a way, is what **Papaji** says, what **Wei Wu Wei** says. And **Cartier-Bresson** goes on: 'Like an orgasm. There's a moment when its bursts.' This, in a way, is **Osho.**

See the connection, the Oneness. Drop dogma. We can revolutionise the quality of our lives with this consciousness. Drop the 'I':

> stuck to the slab
> the   i
> of the frozen f sh

David Steele

———⌇⌇⌇———

The haikuist is not a Quietist ... Dropping the 'I' or deciding to use it in lower case should not be a stylistic decision that is made when drafting or rewriting a haiku. 'Oh, I'll say that differently and drop the I'. No. The 'I' should not be there in the first place – not in true haiku, that is to say, haiku in its purest form. And who wants impure haiku, impure anything? By being in the world, disappearing in the haiku moment – the sacred stream of time, as **Hackett** says – returning only to disappear again in successive haiku moments, the haikuist enjoys the physical and spiritual benefits of Quietism without retreating from the world:

> the damsel fly leaving
>   the lily again and again
>   only to return

Tom Clausen

Haiku is entering the world, the visible world, the invisible world, the world of light and shade:

A crane walks forth
into the brightness that is called
the start of winter

Kagiwada Yūko

―⁓―

The flow of coming and going … The haikuist is at the centre of an
incessant flow of coming and going, a vortex of sights and sounds and is
tuned into the invisible laws which govern all phenomena:

Spring thaw—
names on the gravestones
reappear

Michael Meyerhofer
(*World Haiku Review,* Dec. 2003)

These moments flow whether we are aware of them or not. Awareness
simply gives us a haiku opportunity:

petals
from an unseen cherry tree
drift past my window

Robert Gibson
(*ibid.*)

In such moments of awareness, the vortex can become hushed, still:

cold rain—
a nun's step quietened
by leaves

Alison Williams
(*Blithe Spirit*, Vol. 11, No. 2, June 2001)

Hushed and still. Almost in slumber. And then another rejuvenating
awakening!

how wonderful
    after a long drought
        being a wet hen

Branislava Krzelj

The knowing, observant eye informed by a sympathetic heart:

gorta an gheimhridh
itheann an préachán críonna
    cac na gcaorach

winter hunger
the old crow

gobbles sheep droppings

Cathal Ó Searcaigh
(*Seal i Neipeal*, CIC 2004)

Soberness once more, as the mood dictates, as the silent moment describes itself:

on the river
    a lone gull
        walks the frozen water

Michael Rehling
(*Cherry Blossoms*, River Man Publishing, Sweden, 2003)

—⁓—

Simply looking ... Looking, looking, all the time:

looking at
    one crane
        among ten thousand

Yamada Chiejo
(*Haiku International 1995*)

And where else to go but into the vortex of colour and sound again – and a deep vortex it is too:

from deep within
the rooster crows—
eye glinting

Janice M. Bostok

We can imagine the glint in the haikuist's eye, the eye that sees the invisible taking shape, the inaudible taking sound, the joyous germination of the haiku moment in 'mysterious unity', that same unity alluded to by **Chuang Tzu** in the opening pages of this section.

long winter months
then a robin
brushing against my window

Jocelyne Villeneuve
(*Four Seasons*)

Unthinkable … How unthinkable it would be if we had no robins. Then again, does anyone really know what species of animals, birds and insects are definitely going to survive? As we lose the harbingers of seasons, we also lose something of our relation to the eternal coming and going of phenomena.

⸻

One of the seemingly unstoppable trends in many parts of the world during the twentieth century was the decay of the folkloric mind and a consequent detachment from landscape. How can we relate, as haikuists, to a landscape we inhabit and claim to cherish without repossessing – as much as possible – the nomenclature and lore of flora and fauna? Colonisation can wipe this inheritance away, or distort it, as has happened frequently to place-names:

'I treasure these fond little names when they come into my keeping. From the shores of An Cheathrú Rua, I remember a creek a few feet wide called An Ing Mhór, the big notch, and close by it, An Ing Chaol, the narrow notch, with between them a pinch or two of sand called, believe it or not, An Tráighín Idir Dhá Ing, the little beach between two notches. Would I even have noticed these places strolling by, if they had not been named to me?'

— **Tim Robinson** ("The Seanchaí and the Database, Epiphanies of the Earth," *Irish Pages*, Volume 2, Number 1, Spring/Summer 2003).

The haikuist celebrates the living world. Part of that living world is the accumulated lore which defines its micro-typography. Let us all delve deep into this lore and help to renew its innate vitality.

———

Is this a joke? An anthropologist interviewed an Irish lady, living in the shadow of a mountain. 'Do you believe in the fairies?' She thought about it. 'Personally, sir, I don't believe in them myself. But they're there all the same!'

Poet and haikuist **Cathal Ó Searcaigh** grew up in an Irish-speaking area of Donegal, surrounded by invisible presences:

> 'The other world was adjacent to us and had to be respected; it was necessary to care for the ethereal things and beings that inhabited it. According to my mother, this balance had to be maintained in order to steer us safely through destiny's pitfalls. While she would take the dishwater outside, she would always pause at the threshold for a little while to give the fairies time to get out of the way…'

> (*Trasnú*, 2003)

This cosmology is mirrored in Japan. If a boy was going to urinate in a river, he would first warn the river deities: *'Kawa no kamisama doitokure!'*

———

We see all though none sees us … The fairy literature of Ireland is a calling to the waters and the wild and to a timeless invisible world:

Lovely lady will you go
To that kingdom where stars glow?
    Primrose there the colour of hair
    Snow-white each body fair.

'Yours' and 'mine' are words not known yet,
Ivory teeth and brows of pure jet:
    Foxglove the colour of every cheek,
    The whole company radiant and sleek.

Every plain of purple hue,
The blackbird's eggs flecked with blue,
    The plains of Ireland will seem bare
    After you have lingered there.

For Ireland's beer you will not long,
The Great Land's beer is twice as strong!
     It is a land of purest gold,
     The young don't die before the old.

All round gentle streams entwine,
Mead is drunk, the best of wine;
     The people have not learned to hate,
     It's not a sin to copulate!

We see all on every side
Though none sees us – we do not hide
     But Adam's sin has caused a cloak
     Between us and ordinary folk.

Woman, if you come with me,
On your head a crown will be,
     Fresh pork, the finest ale
     Await us now beyond the pale.

Anonymous (Ireland, 9th century)
(*Treasury of Irish Love*, Ed. Gabriel Rosenstock, Hippocrene Books, New York, 1998)

Genius is not qualitatively different from mere talent. A genius is simply one who has gone beyond the pale of visibility, boldly into the invisible plain of infinite potential.

Have historians ignored imaginative literature and neglected the possibility of there being more than one Shangri-La on this earth? **Morgan Llywelyn** says of the fairy race, the Tuatha Dé Danann, that 'they disappeared into the warp and woof of this island and interpenetrated the very soul of Ireland, never to depart.' (Correspondence with author).

na daoine maithe, an ea?
tá an áit dubh leo . . .
sceach gheal faoi bhláth

νεράιδες, είναι;
γέμισε ο τόπος . . .
ασπραγκαθιές ανθίζουν

(Sarah Thilykou)

fairies, is it?
the place is thick with them . . .
whitethorn in bloom

Did Einstein believe in fairies? Before rubbishing the invisible worlds, let us remind ourselves that **Einstein, Pauli, Planck** and others assure us that the visible tangible world is only a fraction of the universal drama. **Einstein** tells us: 'The most beautiful thing we can experience is the mysterious. It is the source of all true art and all science.' What the literature of the Celtic Otherworld teaches us is nothing more than an elaboration or mythicisation of the haiku moment, namely the miraculous fusion of time and space.

How natural and yet how mysterious it was that the Hopi saw the Earth as being pregnant in Spring. So as not to cause her undue discomfort, they removed the steel shoes from their horses.

—∞—

Be not discouraged ... Let's get back to the world we know...

The world we know? The haikuist must sometimes rub his eyes. Am I really seeing this?

> rubbing my eyes
> over and over again—
> New Years' morning

Toshio

illusion of bloom—
silvery sun
on each magnolia bud

GR

—∞—

Many people become attracted to haiku – especially when they find out what true haiku really is and the difference it can make to our lives. Initially, it looks quite easy. They try their hand at it – as they should – and are satisfied with what it promises. Or they may attend workshops and polish their craft, or send haiku for professional assessment, or are lucky enough to avail of and learn from a master's editing and shaping of their work. But then, something happens. They become discouraged. Their haiku seems to stay on a mental level, not flowing as it should, not flowing every day.

185

Autumn wind—
unless written
words fade away

Asuka Nomiyama
(*Japanese Haiku 2001*, Modern Haiku Association)

———

It can be the same with anything, with martial arts:

'Gurukkal Govindankutty Nayar and his advanced students flowed like a river when they performed their serpentine, graceful, yet powerfully grounded movements. It seemed an unapproachable state of embodiment. When I began my own training in 1976, my body did anything *but* flow…'

(*When the Body Becomes all Eyes: South Indian Martial Art*, Phillip B. Zarrilli, Oxford University Press, 1998).

go further on
says a guide-post
in a withered field

Yamaguchi Soku
(*Haiku International 1995*)

———

Wisdom of doubting … Even those who have written haiku for a number of years – according to **Bashō**, you are a master if you have written ten good haiku in a lifetime – even such people can be distracted by doubt. What's the point of it all? Am I fooling myself? Is this for real?

There's nothing wrong with doubt. It's quite natural. Here's a Zen saying to comfort you: 'Great doubt gives rise to great awakening; small doubt, small awakening; no doubt, no awakening.'

———

Mind to breath … Believing that haiku is easy is a mistake. Thinking that disappearing is easy is a mistake. To approach haiku with the mantra 'First thought, best thought!' is not a bad approach, but it's not quite as easy as it looks. To concur with our opening remarks about 'effortless action' being the key to happiness and success is not far off the mark. But, paradoxical as it may seem, effortless action may require some effort – at first. Reviewing *Spontaneous Mind: Selected Interviews, 1958 – 1996* by **Allen Ginsberg** (Harper Collins 2001) **William Deresiewicz** reminds us that spontaneity isn't always as effortless as it may appear. '"First thought, best thought" was his governing principle: no heed to the high-modernist idea of poem as patiently-constructed artefact, but as an equally strenuous discipline, for it was only with hours of daily meditation that he maintained his wide-open path from mind to breath…' (*New York Times Review of Books*, April 8, 2001).

—⁓—

Creativity: A brief self-dialogue …

Q: You have written a book called *Haiku Enlightenment.* Do you consider yourself to be enlightened?

A: Who is asking the question?

Q: Well, actually, the questioner/responder – you, as it happens.

A: You should know by now that I don't listen to you.

Q: Why not?

A: Why should I? You are the Ghost of Duality Past.

Q: Look at the question again, please…

A: If you insist. I'm looking… It starts by saying, 'You have written a book…' I haven't.

Q: You haven't? Who wrote it then?

A: It must have written itself. With the help of cosmic intelligence.

Q: How?

A: How? Why? What? For whom? Why are you always asking questions?

Q: Because—

A: Just shut up and listen for a while.

Q: To whom?

A: To what, you mean. Listen to anything. There are many sounds in the universe. Listen to whatever you hear now.

Q: I'm listening…

A: To the sound of your own voice! Are you sure you are listening?

Q: It's you that's asking the questions now.

A: Funny, isn't it?

Q: Should I laugh?

A: If it helps you to relax, yes. Please do.

Q: Look, answer the question.

A: Who is asking?

Q: Oh, I give up.

A: That's a start.

Q: Hold on! Just a minute! You have included a section entitled *The Gentle Art of Disappearing*. Have you ever actually disappeared?

A: I'm disappearing now…

Q: You are? Hello?

A: Oh, good! So are you! See you around!

Q: ?

A: !

Q: You are very prolific, Mr Rosenstock. What is the secret of creativity?

A: Oh, you're back! Where have you been?

Q: Here, there and everywhere.

A: Good! Creativity, you say? Try emptying the mind. Have you tried Transcendental Meditation? Have you read **Ashtávakra**?

Q: Who?!

A: Listen, please, very carefully; I'm not going to say it again. This is your chance! You, yourself – your self – you are limited; but you, your Self – are unlimited. That's the secret of creativity. **Papaji** says, 'Find your Self – the treasure – and then distribute it. It is an infinite treasure, and the more you give, the more it will multiply…' That has been my experience. The Self, itself, is the very cradle of creativity.

Q: Wow!

A: Who is saying Wow? Wow wow! You sound like a dog. Stop barking. Be still. Know thy Self.

In the Words of Papaji

> "In order to be born as a baby you have to spend nine months getting bigger and bigger. For Enlightenment you have to get smaller and smaller until you disappear completely."

———

Disappearing! How is it done? There is a word in haiku aesthetics which means slenderness. It is *hosomi*, a delicate quality much favoured by **Bashō**. It is something we can develop in ourselves and in our work, allowing us to enter thin spaces, to follow the spider into its crevice, the bee into its hive, the wren into its nest, the wisp of cloud into a misty lake.

Follow the fall of a dewdrop. Flow! And 'be so little that the elves can reach to whisper in your ear' **(Shelley)**. With *hosomi* we can become creatures of the elements, of the air, of light. Follow the rabbit into its burrow. What is stopping you? You may say, 'But I am not a world philosopher such as **Nishida**, an eccentric monk such as **Ikkyu** or a medieval holy woman or holy man such as **Hildegard von Bingen** or **Jan van Ruysbroeck.**' Maybe not. But nobody expects you to be a philosopher or saint.

Are you essentially any different from haikuists who have been blessed with the haiku moment, whether Japanese, American, Irish, Croatian, Romanian … or those who call themselves citizens of the world? Of course not! We have outlined the dynamics of the haiku moment in *Haiku Enlightenment*. Complete the story. Disappear!

———

Lifting the veils of the self … In a fantastic interview with **Jean Houston** we read about something which could apply to haiku enlightenment: 'I'd say it's an extraordinary effort of reweaving the self in body, mind and spirit that can be accomplished by a depth of loving, by a giving over of the local self to the godstuff. It is the honing of one's inner and outer perceptions so that one is able to see, hear, touch, taste, feel and intuit the immensity of what is really there. The veils of the self are lifted…'[2] Worth pondering that!

———

---

[2] ©*Moksha Press, 1999. This interview first appeared in the Spring/Summer 1999 issue of* What is Enlightenment? *Magazine, entitled "The Self Masters: Are They Enlightened?" and appears by permission of the publisher.*

The (w)hole story ... Meditating on the holed sculptures of **Barbara Hepworth**, the writer **Jeanette Winterson** had this to say: 'A Hepworth hole is not only a connection between different kinds of form, or a way of giving space its own form – it is a relationship with the invisible. Since human beings began their journey towards consciousness, we have sought a relationship with the invisible...'

Put in another way, when the mind is purged of everything else but the intuitive, interpenetrative perception of the *Ding an sich*, the mysterious, pulsating thing-in-itself, the haiku moment of disappearance occurs. For one precious instant, there is no room for you or your thoughts. The rose, the moon, the steaming dunghill fill the world in full flow. **John Muir** says: 'Everything is flowing – going somewhere, animals and so-called lifeless rocks as well as water. Thus the snow flows fast or slow in grand beauty-making glaciers and avalanches; the air in majestic floods carrying minerals, plants, leaves, seeds, spores, with streams of music and fragrance... While the stars go streaming through space pulsed on and on forever like blood ... in Nature's warm heart.'

> bleak February morning
> a white cat declares itself
> in silence

GR

—◦◦◦—

Elusive silence ... We can disappear in silence, when the chattering mind falls silent, when the haiku moment emerges, when we no longer have opinions.

All of us seem to have an opinion on this and that, whether we know all the facts or not. Most of us give too much weight to opinion. We look to the so-called opinion formers in society; our idle chatter and our serious conversations and debates are riddled with opinions.

We seem to forget that our opinions are bound to change and that, we, in time, will question their validity. What were those opinions we once had? Who was the person who held to them? The opinionated self disappears on the haiku path.

For **Angelus Silesius**, the ten thousand things become one, disappear in the All:

So many droplets in the sea, in bread so many grains;
So too of our multiplicity, nothing but God remains

Angelus Silesius

It comes as a relief, along the haiku path, to be opinionless. **Silesius** says:

*Die Meinungen seind Sand, ein Narr der bauet drein
Du baust auf Meinungen, wie kanstu weise sein?*

Opinions are sand, a fool builds on such lies
You build on opinions, how can you be wise?

Angelus Silesius

Forget 'Meinungen & Deinungen', forget mine and thine'. **John W. Sexton** dropped his opinion-forming mind to become completely free of opinion in this haiku:

> sunlit street
>> a jackdaw shadow
>>> passes through me

John W. Sexton
(*Shadows Bloom,* Doghouse, 2004)

—⁓—

Time to disappear ...

> about to vanish
>> in the morning sky
>>> orphaned moon

GR

After all, how long does visibility last before returning to the void?

Autumn morning—
> river-mist rising
> and sheep's breath

Norman Darlington
(*World Haiku Review* 2003)

And for us, too – for all of us, you and I, the cat and the moon, the buffalo's breath in winter, the sheep's breath in autumn – will come a time…

empty fleeting years all gone
now quivering and frail
I must fade away

Ryokan

finally the maple leaf
is at one
with its shadow

Alexis Rotella
(Four Seasons)

Tossed here and there … The early Celts, intimately connected with the natural and the supernatural worlds and had pithy, haiku-like ways of expressing the notion of temporality, of appearance and disappearance:

y ddeilen hon, neus cynired-gwynt
gwae hi o'i thynged;
hi hen, eleni ganed

this wind-tossed leaf
alas its fate: it is old
it was born this year

Anonymous (Wales, 9th century)

flag-covered coffin:
the shadow of the bugler
slips into the grave

Nick Virgilio
(Selected Haiku, 1988)

Desire and disappearance … If you step on this path and fail to disappear – listen to this. If you are sincere enough, a haiku master – living or dead – will emerge to assist you. A dilettante will have little time for you – and possibly see you as a potential rival. A real haiku master will bring you to where he or she is – which is everywhere and nowhere.

there must be light
>   where they came from
>   chestnut blossoms!

GR

"As a drop of water falling on the desert sand is sucked up immediately so we must become nothing and nowhere … we must disappear."

Bhai Sahib

The eternal Being is that state where you have disappeared…

Thayumanavar (1706 – 1744)

heat shimmers
>   an old cyclist
>   rides into infinity

GR

Kakua stood before the emperor in silence. He then produced a flute from the folds of his robe, and blew one short note. Bowing politely, he disappeared…

(*Zen Flesh, Zen Bones: A Collection of Zen and Pre-Zen Writings*, Paul Reps and Nyogen Senzaki)

Haiku Enlightenment

THE UNIVERSAL SPIRIT OF ISSA

The most beautiful thing we can experience in life is the mysterious.

Albert Einstein

Picking up a book called *Writing and Enjoying Haiku* by **Jane Reichhold** (Kodansha International, 2002) one notices dozens of references to **Bashō** in the index and not one reference to **Issa**. It's as if **Issa** has been stuck with the 'country bumpkin' label instead of being acknowledged as one of the three pillars of the haiku world.

In **Makoto Ueda's** *Dew on the Grass: The Life and Poetry of Kobayashi Issa* (Brill, 2004) we read: 'His poetry is lacking in the viewpoint that transcends time and space.' I fail to see the truth of this statement. I am constantly drawn to **Issa** precisely because he transcends, over and over again, the particularities of his own time and space and gloriously so in the following haiku:

> falling from my heart
> the snows
> of Shinano

> *óm chroíse*
> *a thiteann*
> *sneachta Shinano*

When I receive the *Daily Issa*[3] email service from **David Lanoue**, I gaelicise those haiku that hit the spot, that transcend time and space for me. This is my spontaneous personal response to the burst of light which **Issa** releases for me. Then I often do a back translation, that is to say I translate my Irish into English, and this delightful activity keeps me out of pubs and prisons.

The snows in the above haiku are as universal as *The Snows of Kilimanjaro* and deserve to be as famous as the snows of that short story or any other snows you care to mention. The above snow-haiku is a miraculous encapsulation of that most desired quality in haiku, and in life, interpenetration. This is not something you can fake. This is not something you can manufacture. It's a gift. **Issa** had it. His gift was great. There is more than interpenetration at work here. This is pure non-duality, the

---

[3] *Haiku of Kobayashi Issa website, curated by David Lanoue*

internal world and the external world fused as one. This is, manifestly, a transcendence of time and space. It is the stopping of time. The snows are falling from **Issa's** heart. They will do so forever. Universally.

> goose, wild goose
> what was the beginning
> of your journey

> *a ghé, a ghé fhiáin*
> *cén tús*
> *a bhí le d'aistear?*

Here we see the child-like universal quality of wonder which characterises great haiku and great art across many genres. But it expresses more than idle wistfulness, of course. **Issa**, it seems to me, had the great gift of cosmic intelligence. He may not have had as much education or sophisticated insights of a **Buson** or a **Bashō**; nevertheless, he instinctively knew what all the great writers of the world, writers of immense stature such as **Shakespeare** or **Goethe**, were constantly seeking to plumb, the very nature and meaning of existence itself. What was the beginning of your journey, he asks. But this endearing naivety hides a tremendous, a frightening profundity. What **Issa** is really doing in this great haiku is looking at the Self. He is engaging in what Advaita asks us to do, Self-Enquiry, in meditating upon the Self, in abiding in the Self, in knowing that in fact the Self is beginningless and therefore endless. **Yeats** said, 'I am looking for the face I had before the world was made.' Precisely. And **Osho's** epitaph? 'Osho, never born, never died.' And we have it here in **Issa**, in his contemplation of the goose and it is utterly, utterly wonderful! He manages to do it, quite simply, because his heart is open – to the goose and to himself. This is the key. He could easily have closed his heart. By keeping it open, haiku flowed.

Issa knew what he was doing. He was a conscious poet, dedicated to the life of a poet. No other life was possible for him and even when weakened by a stroke there was a palanquin there for him from which he could observe the world. He says in his journal, 'A wandering poet can't help being what he is any more than can a wave that breaks on the shore. His time is short, like foam that disappears in a minute.' Thus the name he gave himself, **Issa** – the feathery foam in a cup of tea. Blink and it's gone. And the haiku moment, how fleeting it is.

> the body of the Buddha
> accepts it—
> winter rain

> *glacann colainn*
> *an Bhúda léi—*
> *báisteach an gheimhridh*

We see the cosmic mind at work again in this sobering haiku, the universal in the particular. I would argue that **Issa's** prolific output is due to one thing and one thing only, namely that he was charged with a cosmic battery, that he was in tune with the infinite, that all things were alive and full of grace and majesty to him, even the lowliest forms of life – especially the lowliest forms of life.

children
don't torment that flea!
she has offspring

*a pháistí
ná ciapaigí an dreancaid sin
tá clann uirthi*

Were children to recite this haiku every day, bullying might disappear. Once bullying disappears, you never know… wars might become unacceptable!

Let's get back to the **Buddha** and the rain. The body of the **Buddha** accepts the winter rain. Of course it does. It accepts everything. The **Buddha** became enlightened not for me or you but for everybody and everything. And, subtly, **Issa** gives the initiated reader a hint that says: so with the **Buddha**, so with **Issa**. He, too, accepts the winter rain. He does not argue with it. How can he? Chilling though the winter rain may be, it is charged with divine energy, divine grace. It is rain, a universal gift and a necessity for life. *Uisce na spéire* it's sometimes called in Irish, sky-water. Haiku is a blessed bridge between heaven and earth, between stillness and movement.

Rain and now snow:

from the east, from the west,
from the south, from the north,
driving snow

*anoir, aniar,
aneas, aduaidh . . .
caidhleadh sneachta*

Issa sees through the driving snow, he sees it coming from all directions, because our country bumpkin has a vantage point, the vantage point of cosmic intelligence. The evidence for this is insurmountable but we may not have seen what was there before our eyes. We may have been fooled into thinking that **Issa** wrote nothing other than charming, amusing and sometimes sentimental haiku, much appreciated by children. Lucky children to have such a Master! **Issa** is a Master like none other. It is not that I am extrapolating layers of meaning that are not really there. They are there, most assuredly, to the sympathetic eye.

> he closes the door
> and goes to sleep . . .
> a snail

> *dúnann an doras*
> *is titeann dá chodladh . . .*
> *slimide*

What is he saying here, that he too switches off sometimes? No, it seems to me that an enlightened master is always awake and the more I absorb **Issa** the more it strikes me that he was, in fact, an enlightened master. For all his travails and hardships, his spirit was free:

> a light heart
> floating through this world . . .
> a pale blue butterfly

> *croí éadrom*
> *ag eitilt tríd an saol seo . . .*
> *féileacán bánghorm*

Many such haiku could be said to form part of a spiritual autobiography. Look at the interpenetration we have in the following haiku:

> she looks at him
> straight in the eye—
> departing goose

> *stánann sí idir an dá shúil*
> *ar an bhfear—*
> *gé ag imeacht*

What a moment in time, captured forever. The universality of this haiku is in its grasping the reality of time, of change, of movement, of seasonality; but as the Indian non-dualist sage, **Papaji**, once said, 'We do not seize Reality; Reality seizes us.' (I have quoted this before and it's worth quoting again). Time and time again, Reality seizes **Issa** and he tells us what it's like, this hair-raising confrontation with what is real, with what it feels like to be awake, to be looked straight in the eye by a goose that's about to depart. It's full of mystery as well. There is something ineffable about this strange encounter between man and bird, yet wonderfully real for all that.

Reading **Issa**, we get a strong feeling of an awakened one, of someone who doesn't wish to drift off into fanciful worlds:

200

gobble up
my dawn dream
cuckoo

tabhair slogadh na lachan
do thaibhreamh seo bhreacadh an lae
a chuaichín

His pure response to the pure call of the cuckoo is that the bird might, as it were, gobble up all his fantasies, dreams and illusions and leave him only with the purity of the beginner's mind.

in a perfect square
the snow on the gate
disappearing

leánn uaim
ina chearnóg fhoirfe
sneachta an gheata

The endless coming and going of phenomena, the appearance and the disappearance of generation after generation, of civilisation after civilisation. It's all in **Issa** if you look. He tells it as it is. The snow. And the melting of the snow. We don't get one without the other. **Issa** wants us to have a full picture. The picture given above, 'in a perfect square the snow on the gate disappearing' would, I think have been appreciated by Dutch artist and Theosophist, **Piet Mondrian**.

the first blanket of snow
all in rags . . .
crows

an chéad bhrat sneachta
ina scifle . . .
préacháin

Nothing sentimental about that, is there? It's not quite nature 'red in tooth and claw' but hints at it nicely. In English poetry, such as *London Snow* by **Robert Bridges**, we often find a picture-postcard view of nature:

When men were all asleep the snow came flying,
In large white flakes falling on the city brown,
Stealthily and perpetually settling and loosely lying,
Hushing the latest traffic of the drowsy town . . .

A different sensibility is at work in the haiku of the Japanese master. We do not necessarily have to prefer one to the other. Each has its special qualities.

What **Bridges** tries to achieve is something similar to **Walter de la Mare's** poem, *Snow:*

> No breath of wind,
> No gleam of sun,
> Still the white snow
> Whirls softly down
> Twig and bough
> And blade and thorn
> All in an icy
> Quiet, forlorn . . .

But I could not read **Bridges** or **Walter de la Mare** repeatedly, over a lifetime. **Issa** I can. The best of his haiku never get stale, not for me at any rate, and it is because his haiku emerge not from some imaginative, atmosphere-building fiction but from the depths (or heights) of Reality itself.

Furthermore, each glimpse of Reality is as real as the next:

> flowering rape—
> and looking west
> Zenko Temple

> *an ráib faoi bhláth—*
> *agus nuair a fhéachaim siar*
> *Teampall Zenko*

> harvest moon—
> and looking west
> Zenko Temple

> *gealach an fhómhair—*
> *agus nuair a fhéachaim siar*
> *Teampall Zenko*

Such close similarity between two poems would be intolerable to poetry lovers. Mainstream poetry would, rightly, see it as a form of self-plagiarism. Not so in haiku. Because it is Reality that matters. And nothing is as universal as Reality, Reality that reflects nature, the spirit of nature, human nature, animal nature:

> he sneaks off
> to where fowlers are scarce—
> the fox

> *ag imeacht san áit*
> *ar gann iad na sealgairí éan —*
> *an sionnach*

Issa's sympathy is with the fox, of course, but in a way it's with everything and everybody, even the bird hunters. What I like about this haiku is its connectedness to the earth, to landscape, to the ways of the land. One of the problems we encounter in the haiku world today is that city haikuists often bend over backwards to argue for the validity of urban haiku. Urban haiku existed in **Issa's** time but he reminds us that in the area of the old capital, Edo, even the scarecrows are crooked! So be warned!

There may be a sneaking admiration in the above haiku for the wily old fox; after all, **Issa** was not the best at handling his worldly affairs. But even the fox doesn't always get his own way:

> hail stones
> driving him crackers—
> the fox

> *imithe le gealaigh*
> *ag na clocha sneachta—*
> *sionnach*

Poets such as **Robert Bridges** and **Walter de la Mare** rely on stock devices – rhyme, rhythm, onomatopoeia and so on – devices which the haiku usually shuns. Avoiding these imaginative layers of beguiling ornamentation and suggestion, dispensing even with a title, the haiku relies solely on the pure shock of Reality.

We must talk now about fleas: they too are part of Reality, of the scheme of things. Let's revisit the flea haiku above:

> children
> don't torment that flea!
> she has offspring

This is not, I would argue, an example of anthropomorphism. Of course a flea has offspring, otherwise how do fleas come into being? **Einstein** says, 'Until he extends his circle of compassion to all living things, man will not himself find peace.' **Issa's** sympathy for fleas, frogs and baby sparrows is often interpreted as simply amusing or touching. It is much, much greater than that. The flea-haiku is a statement of universal compassion. Only someone who was taunted or excluded, or witnessed exclusion, could write such an effective haiku which is nothing short of a plea from the heart for all cruelty, mindlessness and aggression to end.

Issa's enlightenment is found in the balance of rest and activity:

settling down again
in gentle stillness
geese in the rice fields

ag socrú síos arís
sa chiúnas séimh
géanna na ngort ríse

Sublime! It's almost a call to meditation. It is universal in the sense that rest and activity is the lot of all beings. The scene is described on the cusp of serenity, so to speak. The geese are settling down again, which is not the same as some seconds earlier when all is commotion, or some seconds later when the geese are reposing: we actually catch a glimpse of them in motion, settling down to motionlessness. This is superb interpenetration, the spirit, the inner eye following the dynamics of a fleeting moment, becoming that fleeting moment itself and the stillness thereafter.

Actually, we might say that its fleetingness is precisely what demands spontaneous alacrity from the *haijin,* a response which is more than perception, or mere observation, and it is this which creates the haiku moment.

Certainly **Issa** had his sorrows and travails but throughout his body of haiku great joy issues forth as from a fountain:

even the radishes
in the field blooming . . .
the lark singing!

na raidisí fiú
ag bláthú sa ghort . . .
an fhuiseog ag ceiliúradh

This is the spontaneous often unexpected ecstasy experienced by poets and mystics universally and it can visit any of us, at any time, when we are at one with Creation. There is nothing to be sought, to be desired; listen to the delicious sermon of the radishes, that's all, and the heavens will open in song.

And even in a more sombre mood, **Issa** is saying ... what can be added? This is enough beauty, enough happiness for any man:

looking at the mountain
looking at the sea . . .
autumn evening

ag breathnú ar an sliabh
ag breathnú ar an muir . . .
tráthnóna fómhair

The gaze, the untroubled gaze, stretching into infinity, at one with the nature of the Self and the universe. The simplicity of it all. I'm sure it unnerves quite a lot of people! It's strange how people react differently to a handful of syllables. Some enter the mood immediately. It's more than a mood, of course. Others are untouched, unmoved.

I find myself being transformed by reading favourite haiku. It's not easy to describe. As I said above, it's more than a mood. It's not like being injected with a mood-altering substance. It is really an awakening. Something of the quality of dreams colours our perceptions and a good haiku is like a splash of water from a cool mountain stream that wakes us up from our doze. *Looking at the mountain/looking at the sea.../autumn evening.* A universal experience, timeless, and ever new. The act of making a haiku is a celebration of pure consciousness. Thousands of millions of people have gazed at a mountain, have gazed at the sea. But with what degree of consciousness, of awareness, of perception and interpenetration? The haiku opens up all our channels of perception to take in the mystery of mountain and sea, the soul of the mountain and sea; the haiku act is an act of interpenetration, a kind of celibate eroticism!

And from vast vistas back to minutiae again:

> licking spring rain
> from a bamboo leaf . . .
> mouse

> *báisteach earraigh*
> *ar dhuille an bhambú*
> *á lí ag luch*

In the last line of the Irish version, *á lí ag luch*, you can actually hear the little tongue lapping up the droplets of rain as the 'l' sounds imitate the action of the tongue. And this is the great gift of haiku, and **Issa's** wonderful gift to us. He shares with us his blessed witnessing of the unfolding of life in myriad ways; most of these revelations are quite ordinary and reveal how extraordinary the ordinary is. We are there with the mouse. It is the mouse, not a pop star or president, that is centre stage, for a few seconds. That little mouse has been immortalized by **Issa** in a manner which may well outlive **Mickey Mouse**.

Issa's boundless creativity is such that he is naturally in tune with the thousand and one creations and recreations that are going on all around him all of the time, from season to season, year in, year out, and he never tires of these daily miracles:

little chestnuts
pissed on by the horse . . .
    shiny new

castáin bheaga
ar mhún an capall orthu . . .
ag glioscarnach, úrnua

This is a strikingly fresh metaphor for what is going on inside **Issa** himself.
His seeing the world through haiku-vision means that he, too, is being
subtly altered and refined by all that he sees and hears, all that he smells,
touches and feels. He is walking the haiku path, ceaselessly, living and
expressing the haiku creed which is nothing but life itself in its never-
ending game of decay and renewal. Indeed, **Issa** saw not only change
around him but metamorphosis. He says in his journal (*Oraga Haru*):

'No sooner has the snow of last year disappeared in summer than the
first frosts of autumn have come. All the trees not native to this place
but brought in from better climates undergo some changes. The
mandarin orange tree shrinks to half its natural size...'

I love this observation ... the shrinking tree; it's almost a metaphor for
haiku itself.

the life of a snail
he goes to bed and gets up
    just the way he is

beatha an tseilmide
téann a luí agus éiríonn
díreach mar atá sé

This is priceless! Haiku's compactness makes it wonderfully suitable to
handling small things. Not that haiku couldn't handle a herd of elephants, of
course it could. But there's something exquisitely charming about those
haiku of his that deal with frogs, fireflies, fleas and snails. 'The life of a
snail/he goes to bed and gets up/ just the way he is'. Just the way he is,
that's great. As if he could be any other way. And **Issa** says that the way he
is cannot but be perfectly fine. 100%. Just the way he is! And so it is...

This identification with snails and the like is also a form of self-
effacement. The sage with the Chinese name (whose father was High
Sheriff of Armagh, God help us!), **Wei Wu Wei**, observed that a saint is
someone who disciplines the ego and a sage is one who drops it.

beginning of Spring—
sparrows at the gate
with their little faces

tús an earraigh—
gealbhain ag an ngeata
gona n-aghaidheanna beaga

206

Issa observes the sparrows at the gate and then his heart goes out to them on seeing their little faces. It is the heart that sees. He might have had his head in the clouds a lot of the time but **Saint Exupéry** got it right when he said something very similar: 'It's only with the heart that one sees rightly.' **Issa** saw with the heart, the universal heart of man. Paternal-maternal. He saw with the heart like none other. But it is not the way of the world, alas, to see with the heart. And that is why **Issa's** world stature is not as great as it should be.

Let's go back to Zenko Temple:

faces looking like
they've been to Zenko Temple
    baby sparrows

is cosúil go rabhadar
i dTeampall Zenko
aghaidheanna na mionghealbhan

Read this haiku with the purity of mind in which it was composed and we, too, become visitors to Zenko Temple; we, too, acquire the face of a baby sparrow, the eternal innocence of our inherent Buddha nature. The Self cannot be defiled. The mind and the body can know defilement but not the Self. **Issa's** immortal haiku spring from his immortal Self. (Not all of his haiku, of course. He could indulge in trivia as well).

my favourite cormorant
the one who surfaces
    with nothing

an broigheall is gile liomsa
é siúd a thagann aníos
is a ghob folamh!

In parts of the East, they still fish with cormorants, their necks ringed so that they don't swallow the catch, and **Issa's** favourite is the one that comes up with nothing.

In a world obsessed with success, **Issa** teaches us to love a loser. If there isn't a Love a Loser Day, let's have one! 'My favourite cormorant/the one who surfaces/with nothing'. Perfect!

The nothing is also something, of course. As a Buddhist, **Issa** would have contemplated nothing, emptiness, the Void. Nothing is essential! Without nothing there can't be anything. And the Void, *sunyata,* is universal. *The Heart Sutra* tells us form is emptiness, emptiness form. This understanding adds an extra flavour to the cormorant haiku.

Issa's Buddhism can be expressed in pious, traditional terms or equally with a touch of humour. In this haiku we overhear the tea-harvesters:

"Praise Buddha
praise Buddha!"
picking tea-leaves

"*Molaimis an Búda!*
Molaimis an Búda!"
ag piocadh duilleoga tae

The lowliest tasks become impregnated with a celestial flavour. And in the next, an awesome statue of the Buddha makes us smile:

from the esteemed nose
of the esteemed Buddha—
an icicle

ar shrón oirirc
an Bhúda oirirc—
bior seaca

Has the serene beauty of the statue been lessened by the icicle, and caused us to fall from the sublime to the ridiculous? No. The statue is made of stone. The icicle on the other hand is a living thing. Zen-haiku Master **J. W. Hackett** says: 'Remember that lifefulness, not beauty, is the real quality of haiku.' Lifefulness! **Issa** is not lacking in that respect.

when the nightingale
settles in the pine—
the voice of the pine

nuair a lonnaíonn
an filiméala sa ghiúis—
guth na giúise

We keep returning to interpenetration. **Einstein** talked about extending our circle of compassion to all living things. We have concluded that we can do this perfectly by seeing with the heart. We have seen **Issa** to excel in this field, perhaps above all other *haijin.* Look at this:

little chestnuts
how often
you are trampled upon

a chastána beaga
nach mion minic
a shatlaítear oraibh!

My Romanian grandson, Seán, visited us recently and I introduced him to all my friends, including a dog turd. Flies had gathered. 'Say hello to my friends, the poo-flies!" I said to him. He was somewhat astounded by my circle of friends but I think he got the message.

Issa's chestnut-haiku is seeing with a very big heart indeed, into the living heart of the universe:

> *oíche shamhraidh—*
> *tá na réaltaí fiú*
> *ag cogarnaíl lena chéile.*

In **Robert Hass's** translation:

> summer night—
> even the stars
> are whispering to one another!

This is the gift of haiku, of course. It gives a hint, just a hint, but an unmistakeable hint nonetheless, of immensity. To have written such a haiku, there must have been an immensity in **Issa** himself. Whether he was conscious of this immensity or took it for granted is not the central point. His was a great soul, a mahatma, a universal spirit.

The best description I have read concerning the opening of the heart, seeing with the heart and how this might influence our endeavours (artistic and otherwise) came from a Sufi source:

'As one can see when the eyes are open, so one can understand when the heart is open.'

— **Hazrat Inayat Khan**

Now let us look at a commentary on that by **Pir-o-Murshid Inayat Khan**:

'Every name and every form speaks constantly, constantly makes signs for you to hear, for you to respond to, for you to interpret, that you may become a friend of God.'

So far so good as to linking these words with the haiku path, namely, every name and every form constantly speaking, constantly making signs for us to hear, to respond to and to interpret…'

This challenge, which needn't be arduous at all, gives meaning to life. Let's read on:

'How can we grow to read and understand the message that life speaks through all its names and forms? The answer is that, as by the opening of the eyes you can see things, so by the opening of the heart you can understand things. As long as the heart is closed you cannot understand

209

things. The secret is that, when the ears and eyes of the heart are open, all planes of the world are open, all names are open, all secrets, all mysteries are unfolded.'

It must be fairly obvious how this wonderful insight into life can be applied to haiku, to **Issa's** haiku and to the best haiku that came before and after him. **Pir-o-Murshid Inayat Khan** then goes on to ask us how is it done? How do we open the heart, how do we see and understand with the heart?

For the haikuist, for most artists, and for most people, this is the most important question of all, I would suggest:

'The way to it is a natural life, the life of the child, smiling with the smiling one, praying with the praying one, ready to learn from everyone, ready to love. The child has enmity against no one, he has no hatred, no malice, his heart is open. It is in the child that you can see the smiles of angels; he can see through life. When the grown-up person is made ready, when he has acquired the attributes of the child, then he creates heaven within himself, he understands. The child with his innocence does not understand, but when a man with understanding develops the childlike loving tendency, the purity of heart of the child with the desire to be friendly to all – that is the opening of the heart…'

All this applies to **Issa**. The seeing heart of **Issa** saw the cosmos as *leela,* play, and what else was **Issa** to do but enter into this cosmic play with child-like delight. And the result?

'Everything becomes spiritual once this door of the chamber of the heart is open. If a man is a musician, then his music is celestial. If he is a poet, then his poetry is spiritual. If he is an artist, then his art is a spiritual work. Whatever he may do in life that divine spirit manifests. He need not be a religious person, he need not be a philosopher, he need not be a mystic. It is simply that what was hidden in him and thereby was keeping his life incomplete begins to manifest to view, and that makes his life perfect.'

<table>
<tr><td>snow's melting!
and the village overflows . . .
with children</td><td>sneachta ag leá
is an sráidbhaile ag cur thar maoil …
le leanaí</td></tr>
</table>

Haiku Enlightenment

Afterthought

The Art of Emptiness

(Keynote address to Haiku Canada 2015)

What does the moon know of haiku? What does the wind know? The rain? Nothing. And yet they are our teachers, or guides, now and for all time.

What do I know of haiku? Nothing. And it has taken me a long time, I can assure you, to know nothing. Now that I know nothing – which is all one needs to know – why would I desire anything else?

There are so many things we know and so many things we forget; but, knowing nothing, what is there left to shed, to lose, to forget? Haiku is the art of emptiness, of knowing nothing; it is the art of the no-mind, the beginner's mind. The innocent mind.

Knowing nothing is where it all begins and ends, if we can talk about a beginning and an end at all: there is the momentary froth of appearance – a shape, a phenomenon, a colour, a scent, a bubble in **Issa**'s cup of tea[4], and it disappears. And we're left with nothing again, if we're lucky.

True haiku is a celebration of unclutteredness, emptiness, fleetingness, vastness, littleness, nothingness. Bad haiku is a klunky declaration of substance and ego – substance that is awarded the appearance of substantiality when it is, in fact, quite unreal. A shadow chasing a shadow. No more. Maybe we shouldn't talk about good haiku and bad haiku at all. There's haiku and then there's non-haiku.

The world is full of bad haiku (or non-haiku) because the world takes itself so seriously, considering itself to be absolutely real, substantial, solid as a rock, and requiring a constant supply of novels, films, newspapers, philosophical and scientific treatises and so on – even haiku – to describe it, interpret it and guarantee its existence. Bad haiku (non-haiku) is full of stolid, boring, impenetrable objects, glanced at by the lifeless eye.

The path of emptiness leads us to inner spaciousness, immediately or over a lifetime of devotion to the art of emptiness; without this inner spaciousness the world of phenomena cannot be perceived or recorded with the freshness and memorability that good haiku truly demand.

The haikuist (*haijin*) should not attempt to arm himself as a novelist, scientist or journalist does. The *haijin's* art is to pare away, not to fill out or

---

[4] *The pen name **Issa** is a reference to the momentary froth of bubbles in a cup of tea.*

enlarge upon what appears to be large enough already. The *haijin's* art is to discover the breath of abiding nothingness in phenomena, in heat and cold, drought and deluge, light and darkness and shade; the living breath of abiding nothingness; and he can only do that by becoming nothing himself, gradually over a lifetime, or instantly, suddenly, now.

By becoming nothing, stripped of judgements, attachments, we can enter the abiding breath of nothingness, fleeting and eternal. What do these words mean? They can only mean something if they reflect your actual experience of reading and writing haiku. Otherwise, all this is just gobbledegook in an ocean of gobbledegook.

Another word for emptiness is *sunyata* and that was the name of a man who was born in Denmark in 1890. A book, *Dancing with the Void* (Non-Duality Press, 2015) gives us an insight into his innocence, his divine emptiness which is such fertile ground for haiku; not just for haiku but for all the best things in life.

Now, it must be said that reading and writing haiku is a special art, like no other. I have a number of friends and acquaintances and they simply never got it and probably, now, never will – and I'm talking about people from whom I expected more. (Or do I mean less?! Let's not be tempted by wordplay here). Then there are others who surprised me by getting it instantly.

You can't fake it. When someone gets it, you know they've got it. They've been to the boundless realm and drunk the milk of paradise. Three lines of a haiku may look like a shallow rock pool but we know from **Chiyo-ni** that it is alive, tremendously alive and contains more than we know.

> whatever I pick up
> is alive—
> ebbing tide

> **Chiyo-ni**

Over the centuries and in our own time, these little haiku rock pools have managed to reveal the complete depth and majesty of the ocean itself – boundlessness, emptiness, fullness.

The truth of the matter is that when we approach the essence of true haiku, we are forced into making statements that seem self-contradictory – something of the nature of a *koan*, almost – but it is in the apparent shallowness of the haiku form that we find the unknowable depths; it is in the emptiness that we find fullness beyond measure; in the nothingness we find everything, and our own secret core.

How come? Patient, sensitive reading of the haiku masters – and re-reading, of course – can spark off a meditative insight in the reader in which the depth of a haiku is revealed in the reader's own depth, a depth that is sounded in pure, universal consciousness.

This is what makes haiku unique in the literary world. Haiku can subtly transform our awareness of being alive and awaken us from habitual torpor and lassitude. If haiku forms part of your daily activity, whether reading, writing, teaching or translating haiku, my guess is that you will never know what lassitude is. Or torpor. Because those 17-syllables or less (or syllabets, in Japanese), are packed with an espresso-like kick, and a powerful aroma.

I'm not going to analyse the kick of that aroma, or spend much time in suggesting what elements go into a haiku to create this shock of consciousness. Disjunctiveness? Parataxis? Interpenetration? Oh, that's called paralipsis, as many of you may know, drawing attention to something by saying one is not going to talk about it!

An example of parataxis from **Beckett's** *Waiting for Godot:*

'out . . . into this world . . . this world . . . tiny little thing . . . before its time . . . in a god for– . . . what? . . . girl? . . . yes . . . tiny little girl . . . into this . . . out into this . . . before her time . . . godforsaken hole called . . . called . . . no matter'

Parataxis is the lack of conjunctions. We must fill in the empty spaces. **Beckett**, **Pinter**, modern masters of breath, of pause, of emptiness.

As I said, in my paralipsis, I'm not going to dwell on these matters of technique. What is truly important is to know that true haiku catapults us into infinity; it creates an aperture which not only suggests infinity, it actually allows us through, into infinity. Haiku is a portal to emptiness. Those who are afraid to enter may fiddle around with the form of haiku, with words and images, but will never experience the spirit of haiku – impossible – without going through that portal.

Going through that portal is 'a naked moment', to use a term in **Patricia Donegan's** book, *Haiku Mind* (Shambhala Books). **Mahavir**, who said 'Know the moment', Mahavir had only the cloak on his back, which he gave to a beggar, then off he goes into the forest, naked. Through the portal. Empty.

Entering this emptiness need not be a dramatic event. It can be an ordinary event of extraordinary beauty and significance.

Let us taste a haiku now:

the spirit, the truth
of silent prayer —
just the moon on the road

Kikusha-ni (1752-1826)

This haiku has a devotional essence, an attitude that makes it precious and pure, an attitude that today's *haijin* must (re)learn. Once this attitude becomes part of our chemistry, then it becomes easier to experience all phenomena with the beginner's mind, the innocent mind, in silent prayer before mystery. (When I say 'silent prayer,' needless to say I'm speaking of haiku as a form of non-denominational prayer but we can't exclude 'believers' from this experience either). Many of today's *haijin* have the 'wise-guy' mind, the 'clever' mind, the slick mind and there's quite enough of that in the world already.

Haiku today – especially those haiku written in the Anglosphere – lack the spirit of devotion and reverence which I now consider to be vital if haiku is to nourish the soul of writer and reader alike. I don't need haiku to nourish my brain or tickle my fancy. There are other things that do that, even without my asking.

Kikusha-ni, the wandering nun, what did she see when she visited Yoshino?

on the summer hills
I saw a cloud – that's all
there was in Yoshino

Kikusha-ni

To follow her path today – the path of wanderers such as **Santōka** – requires a mindset which **Kaneko Tohta** calls *teijū hyōhaku* or settled wandering.

I take my hat off to **Kikusha-ni**. In these two delicate haiku the spirit of emptiness is embodied in prayerful humility. The wandering nun shows us that the haiku path unfailingly rewards us with the surprise of the new. There is no need for gimmickry or sensationalism – the now is new. It has never been experienced before, arising as it does out of emptiness and its infinite creative potential!

Let us lose ourselves to emptiness, over and over again. There can be no clinging to emptiness. **Dōgen** says:

The track of the swan through the sky
    Never leaves traces—
        Its path is soon forgotten

Dōgen

Let's not forget that the poets and artists most admired by **Bashō** had the
recluse, wandering spirit of **Kikusha-ni**: the Chinese **Li Bai**, **Hanshan** and
Du Fu as well as the Japanese masters of *renku*, *haiga* and the tea
ceremony. We must study the masters and study those masters whom the
masters themselves admired. Then we begin to see into the life of haiku. In
the book *Finding Wisdom in East Asian Classics* by **William Theodore De
Bary** (Columbia University Press) we find a comment on this haiku by
Bashō:

shizukesa ya	how still it is!
iwa ni shmiiru	stinging into the stones,
semi no koe	the locust's trill

Bashō

Our attention is drawn to the frequency of the 'i' vowel in this haiku – the
sound of the locust, or cicada. For me, this sound can be reproduced better
in Irish than in English. English closes off sounds with its consonants. Irish
and Japanese have more going on in terms of vowel music. Here's the Irish
(this is not a subjective thing – the vowels in Irish add more resonance and
echo than is possible in English):

nach ciúin atá sé—
clocha á ndingeadh
ag giolc an chiocáda

I learn from **De Bary** that four versions of **Bashō's** cicada haiku exist and
the sound of the cicada goes from a verb to mean 'seep' to a verb that
means to 'cut' or 'penetrate' or 'sting'. This was an enlightening insight for
me. I felt, rightly or wrongly, that **Bashō** was attempting to cut through
materiality itself, to find and explore the nature of silence and emptiness.
The sound of the cicada travels through the empty air and stabs the rocks,
seeps into them, stings them, cuts through them. And then? It dies in
emptiness. Just as a mantra, that is intoned silently, enters the mind and
subsides therein, in the vast field of emptiness.

Every haiku moment should begin and end with silence.

Let me tell you how I teach haiku – through the grace of the masters. Taking haiku by **Issa**, **Bashō**, **Buson** or lesser-known masters, I ask a participant to write that haiku on a whiteboard, where nothing was before. You could have written that, I say (but you didn't). We look at the haiku for a moment, in silence, and after contemplating its beauty, simplicity, emptiness and depth, we discuss it, a little, and talk about some aspect or another of haiku aesthetics. And then someone is asked to erase the haiku and we're left again with a tabula rasa. Emptiness. And so it goes. Each haiku moment is the birth and death of a moment. We die and are reborn in haiku. This is the truth of haiku but we mustn't become cultish about it!

Let's take another little haiku break now:

picked
   by an old woman's hand
   herbs green and glowing

Soen Nakagawa

I'm often left speechless by such haiku. Wordless. Everything has gone into that haiku, glowingly. Everything! I'm left with nothing… Until the next haiku event and so on in the endless cycle of birth, death and rebirth.

Self-emptying is called 'kenosis' in the Christian tradition and the greatest *haijin* of modern times to embody the spirit of self-emptying was the short-lived **Svetlana Marisova** (1990-2011). This is a haiku she wrote three months before her death:

swan song . . .
   the limb-loosening rush
   of dark feathers

Svetlana Marisova

There is another kind of emptiness in us as well and it is connected with emotion, desire, memory, nostalgia and dream, a gnawing emptiness which haiku can momentarily fill and yet leave us empty again, as in this contemporary Japanese haiku by **Fujiki Tomoko**:

みちのくや身の裡に雪棲みならし

michinoku ya mi no uchi ni yuki suminarashi

> the far north country . . .
> somewhere within myself
> the snow lives on

Fujiki Tomoko

———〜〜〜———

Tobias Wolff's phrase 'synaptic lightning' is a memorable description of what happens in a true haiku. I say 'happens.' Yes. Something is happening, a synaptic lightning and there's nothing happening in real haiku that is not true, occurring now and in the endless realm.

Haikuists are not alone, of course, in their experience of the endless realm. Their experience has been validated by others, not all of them artists, or mystics. *The Endless Realm* is the title of a poem by **Sun Ra** which has these lines:

> Nothing is mine
> How treasured rich am I
> I have the treasure of nothing . . .
> Vast endless nothing
> That branches out in the realm beyond realm . . .

Sun Ra

This type of writing cannot easily be faked. It arises from an experience that shatters barriers. **Emerson**, who hated quotes, is nevertheless one of the most quotable of modern philosophers and he says: 'Let us be silent, that we may hear the whisper of God.'

Haiku create silences, arise from silence, return to silence. How? Haiku shut out the noise of the world in concentrating on pure phenomena – even when such phenomena themselves contain sound. It becomes a silenced sound, a return to the beginning of sound, the first quack of a duck, or the cry of a pheasant that has just swallowed a whole field, the silence before and after that cry.

> swallowing
> the open field—
> pheasant's cry

Yamei
(Ivan M. Granger)

A haiku has the ability to present phenomena with such intensity that we feel something unique is happening. **Emerson** again: 'If the stars should appear one night in a thousand years how would men believe and adore … but every night come out these envoys of beauty, and light the universe with their admonishing smile…'

Had he known about haiku, **Emerson** would, I believe, have championed the form as an important contribution to the world's wisdom literature, for he says, 'The invariable mark of wisdom is to see the miraculous in the common.'

It is so for us too, is it not? I think he would have been pleased to champion haiku. Again, he says:

'Even in the mud and scum of things, something always, always sings.' This is haiku philosophy, as I understand it.

———

What, in recent years, have I learned about haiku? Nothing. Let me expand. On first reading **R. H. Blyth**, my first encounter with haiku, I believe I learned all that I needed to learn, that is to say, I absorbed the essentials, tasted the heart of haiku. Everything else I learned was simply a footnote to that experience, some further exposition of the essentials, some other words, phrases or concepts which elucidated my initial understanding, or refreshed my original initiation.

ancient pond . . .
    a frog jumps
    into the sound of water

      Bashō

Thomas Hoover, for example, commenting on **Bashō's** famous frog haiku: 'To write this type of poem, the artist must completely disengage – if only for an instant – all his interpretive faculties.'

These words simply opened up new ways of re-experiencing and interpreting my first experience of haiku. **Hoover** says that what happens with real haiku is that the *haijin* 'becomes one with the world around him, allowing his craft to operate instinctively…' This makes perfect sense to me and the process is very well described when he says that 'this instantaneous perception moves directly from his senses to his innermost understanding, without having to travel through his interpretive faculties'.

Very well said! Haiku that I enjoy reading (and writing, or translating) follow this electric pattern which **Hoover** describes so insightfully. Those haiku that I read (or write) which do not conform to **Hoover's** description of the event invariably leave me unmoved and disappointed.

Once visited by the grace of haiku – the art of emptiness – there is nothing more to learn because with it comes a vision that is perfect in itself and renews itself. What we learn thereafter is simply some new way of explaining or describing the experience.

Not that **Blyth** is perfect in every way. His dismissal of Shinto as a superstition reflected his inability to disengage from the tenets that informed his own Western upbringing.

OK, I hear you saying – gimme some of this emptiness. 'Some' of this emptiness? It's all or nothing. Fine! How do I do it? By letting go, as **Mahavir** did, letting go of his last stitch. Letting go as the African-American master **Richard Wright** demonstrates:

I am nobody:
A red sinking autumn sun
Took my name away

Richard Wright

For all his insights, **Blyth** never fully managed to let go of his own cultural trappings.

The disciples of **Bashō** were very keen to transmit the precious knowledge imparted to them by their master. One of those disciples, **Hattori Tohō** (1657 -1730) says in *The Red Booklet* something about the spontaneous nature of haiku which is quite fascinating; he says that the haiku must come 'before the illumination of the object disappears'. This is beautifully and sensitively expressed. It suggests to me that the haiku moment is a moment of grace, an illuminated moment, but we only have an instant to know it, to possess it and be possessed by it – the act of interpenetration – and then the illumination fades, disappears. Now! There! You have it, this is it – the secret of secrets. (I'm beginning to sound cultish myself now).

Better take another haiku break. Two haiku by **Geraldine Clinton Little**, a name we seldom if ever hear in her native Ireland:

the shadow
of a single buttercup
reshaped by wind

Geraldine Clinton Little

the white spider
whiter still
in the lightning's flash

Geraldine Clinton Little

—*w*—

With landscape and natural phenomena, we really only get one shot at it – since landscape is alive, not frozen. Responding, as I do, to landscape photography and to works of art, usually from the school of Realism or Impressionism, one *can* get a second chance and, even, a number of chances. I have written different haiku in response to the same photograph by American master photographer **Ron Rosenstock**, a genius at capturing the pervading emptiness and luminosity of landscape.

> 'Go to the pine if you want to learn about the pine, or to the bamboo if you want to learn about the bamboo. And in doing so, you must leave your preoccupation with yourself. Otherwise you impose yourself on the object and do not learn. Your poetry comes naturally when you and the object have become one – when you have plunged deep enough into the object to see its hidden light glowing within.'

> **— Bashō**

Is 'interpenetration' possible with photography as it is with, let us say, the pine tree which **Bashō** singled out in his advice, 'Go to the pine'? Of course it is, when it is the haiku mind, the beginner's mind, the innocent mind that is brought to the photograph. The great **Cartier-Bresson** says that 'the creative act lasts but a brief moment, a lightning instant of give-and-take'. Please, note that! Give and take.

In my green and salad days I was deeply influenced by the images of **Henri Cartier-Bresson**, the French photographer who incidentally was in **Ramana Maharshi's** ashram at the time of the sage's death. **Cartier-Bresson** says lots of things which might be of interest to haiku artists. This for instance: 'The photograph itself doesn't interest me. I want only to capture a minute part of reality.' I find that interesting – and inspiring. As is this: 'To photograph is to hold one's breath, when all faculties converge to capture fleeting reality. It's at that precise moment that mastering an image becomes a great physical and intellectual joy.'

Turning to painting, I would like to recall something said by **Su Shi** (1037-1101): 'In painting bamboos, one must have bamboo formed in one's breast; at the time of painting, one concentrates and sees what one wants to paint. Immediately one follows the idea ... like a hawk swooping down on a rabbit. With a moment's hesitation it would be lost...'

These are the secrets of haiku enlightenment, of the art of emptiness. Please do not take them too seriously. An enlightened being once said that enlightenment is not such a wondrous thing at all – 'it emits less light than a firefly's buttocks!'

I have only very recently started to compose haiku in response to art. I was delighted to discover that the previously mentioned **Geraldine Clinton Little** published haiku responses to 18th century prints by **Suzuki Harunobu** This one was first published in *Haiku Canada* (Vol. 4, No. 4):

heavy with snow – the
pine of a thousand years
and the bamboo shoots

Geraldine Clinton Little

Nishiyama Sōin (1605 -1682), a contemporary and acquaintance of **Bashō** in *One Hundred Buddhist Verses*, says: 'Above all, the way of haiku is to put emptiness first and substance last…' Does the way of haiku – 'emptiness first' – have wider implications other than the author's intentions, which were literary and spiritual, I take it? Yes, why not? 'Emptiness first' can be a critique of the excesses of capitalist consumer culture, for instance.

Haiku is a form of soul travel, from nothingness to nothingness. Masters such as **Onitsura** (1661-1738), who began to learn the art of haiku at the age of eight, have shown the way:

my soul
dives in and out of the water
with the cormorant

Onitsura
(R. H. Blyth)

Unlike other literary forms, the totality of each haiku reverberates back to the reader, and there is a silence and an emptiness at the heart of it.

A haiku by grandmaster **Buson**:

in Matsushima
a man gazing at the moon—
empty seashells

Buson

Is he talking about himself or alluding to **Bashō** who was once so overcome by the moonlight in Matsushima that no words came to him. Empty seashells!

The Victorian era propelled us into the inventiveness that would lead to the technological age and our eventual divorce from the sights, sounds, aromas, silences and rhythms of nature – the very life blood of haiku itself. Victorian inventiveness led to our own age, the Age of Mass Distraction, as it has been called, in which every minute of the day seems to be a conspiracy against silence, as Green Anarchists proclaim. This is not the spirit of **Issa** – **Issa** whose favourite, trained fishing-cormorant was the one that surfaced with his beak … empty.

> my favourite cormorant
> the one who surfaces
> with nothing
>
> **Issa**

The Victorian era ushered in an age of scientific rationalism and Darwinism. What's wrong with Darwinism, you might ask? The Darwinist doctrine is 'the survival of the fittest,' a doctrine which justified the Establishment's indifference to famine in Ireland and India, for instance. This doctrine is not the way of haiku, an art that is imbued with compassion for all things.

Had the age of the machine been informed by the spirit of Shinto then before we might think of discarding and replacing any of our machines – a car, a typewriter, or a computer, say – we would first bow to it, pray to it, thank it for its service and wish it all the best in its new, recycled life to come!

The Victorians were all out to win and win they did, in many ways. The will to win is the culture of our times, in sports, in business, in wars. **Joseph Heller's** dark masterpiece *Something Happened* has the gym master complaining about the narrator's uncompetitive son: 'He has to learn now that he has to be better than the next fellow.' Let's hope that this odious philosophy never infects the haiku community. Once it does, with all its egoic trappings, that's the end of haiku – and the beginning of *my-ku*.

(I know enough about the history of haiku to realise that haiku groups in the past were riddled with rivalry and it's no better today. There's nothing wrong with argumentation and conflicting ideologies – as long as such behaviour falls short of feeding the ego).

Lest I sound like a conservative traditionalist in these matters, there's no reason why *gendai* haiku – all forms of modern, avant-garde haiku – should not exist alongside (but not in place of) haiku as we all know it.

The Victorian ethic seems, to me, to be the opposite of *muyō*, which is Japanese not only for 'emptiness' but also for 'uselessness'. Usefulness, indeed, rather than uselessness, seems to have informed the ideals of Victorian entrepreneurship. Is usefulness compatible with haiku? I doubt it. *Muyō*, emptiness, should inform our lives and our haiku; so, let us all then be *muyōsha*, useless persons. To be an accomplished *muyōsha,* a useless person, has never been very difficult for me. (Ask my wife).

Haiku has been described as a way of life, a way of living. If it is to survive in the West, each generation should remind itself of what that implies. It is more, much more, than a literary pursuit. It is a call to each and every one of us to weave into our lives something of the essence of the *muyōsha*.

> 'A useless monk on a pilgrimage to the western provinces, I know the use of uselessness and the pleasures of pleasurelessness. Without purpose or discriminations, I know only the virtue of good health. Cared for by villagers and spring blossoms, and teased by the autumn foliage, I pass the years wandering wherever my heart and feet may lead me. As for the idle hours of my journey, I fritter them away composing haiku… Above all, the way of haiku is to put emptiness first and substance last.'

> — **Nishiyama Sōin** (Quoted in *The Aesthetics of Strangeness*, W. Puck Brecher, University of Hawai'i Press, 2013)

We have come to the end of our ramblings. The rest is emptiness.

Haiku Enlightenment

ANATOMY OF A HAIKU

Many people lack the patience and the sensitivity to gain real nourishment and pleasure from haiku. It is only by tasting and re-tasting haiku that we can begin to read between the lines and experience a multi-layered effect.

Pure haiku arise from subtle levels, mantra-like, and can have mantra-like effects. It is a curious fact that the author of the *longest* poem in the English language, **Sri Aurobindo**, prophesied that the poetry of the future would be mantric.

I was in Cochin, now called Kochi, in Kerala, Southern India, and was up at five o' clock to catch an early-morning flight. Opening a window, the first glimmer of dawn coincided with the muezzin's call to prayer. Here is the haiku that emerged from that experience:

Allah-o akbar!
>   first light over Kochi
>   trembling waves

GR

One doesn't like to read too much into anything but, for the sake of elucidation, how many strands are actually at work here? Firstly, the muezzin cries out that God is great. The emerging light of dawn is linked with this statement, physically and metaphysically. Already, sound and sight are weaving something new for my brain, a unique moment hitherto unexperienced. The invisible muezzin … his nameless voice.

Syllabically, the haiku amounts to thirteen syllables, the second line being the longest; this is more or less the favoured make-up of today's free-style haiku. Apart from the Arabic, it is in plain enough language. It describes a moment, in time and space. Time of day often replaces the previous requirement of a seasonal reference. It is reasonably euphonious, I hope, without being over-musical. So far so good with our rudimentary analysis.

The trembling waves…. What might they be? We must beware of too subjective an interpretation of any work, even our own, but it is arguable that this haiku is beginning to function on several levels. Trembling waves could easily refer to waves on the sea. Kochi, after all, is a port city (with an old synagogue). A typical device, which a haikuist often draws upon without intentionality, is to introduce a complementary image which resonates with the first image, though not necessarily having an obvious association. (Many authors believe that such a device is, indeed essential: see *The Poetics of Japanese Verse,* Kōji Kawamoto, University of Tokyo Press, 2000)

Waves could also refer to sound waves, the voice of the muezzin. Waves might also conceivably refer to waves of light, light waves of the dawn. The waves of creation itself? Echoes of the Big Bang? Now now, let's get a hold of ourselves here!

Yes, one can explain details, in a logical or in an intuitive manner, in hindsight, things which were mysteriously and seamlessly one at the time of the haiku moment or its composition in words. But, isn't the Big Bang going a wee bit too far? Not really. Doesn't astronomy and cosmic physics teach us that compression ultimately leads to an unbelievable expansion? And what is haiku but compression par excellence? (Okay, maybe I am overstating my case – it is simply as an anecdote and as a reaction to those who see nothing at all in a haiku!)

And trembling? Trembling could suggest something of the fear of God, God's greatness, conveyed by the haunting voice that cuts through the early morning stillness. However, as it was written at the beginning of 2004, is there not the possibility that – subconsciously at least – 'trembling' also suggests the pathological fear of Muslim culture which has become part of our world's neurosis today? Or is 'trembling waves' nothing more than pathetic fallacy, a much-used device in Gaelic poetry? Is it the "I" that trembles? Before what? Itself? Before the power of monotheism? If so, what spurs this trembling? Fear? Loathing? Alienation? Ineffable admiration and awe?

———

I give all of these possible meanings – and allow for more – with the express intention of showing that a real haiku – as opposed to a pseudo-haiku – is not a slight thing at all. Over the years the appearance of much bad haiku has relegated haiku to the status of an amusing poetic aside within the popular imagination.

We know it can be more than that, much more. It is up to the reader to complete the jigsaw with his own understanding and experience of what is real.

Of course, I was not mentalizing on these various levels and interpretations when the actual event happened. I was drawn into the web of sound, into tendrils of light, disappearing in their interstices. **Rousseau** says:

'I feel an indescribable ecstasy and delirium in melting, as it were, into the system of beings, in identifying myself with the whole of nature…'

Every haiku moment is a gift from the Invisible, the Unknown – and every haiku that is written is a returning of that gift to the Invisible, to the Unknown. Otherwise there would be a clutter.

Issa wrote over 20,000 haiku – he received over 20,000 thousand gifts. He gave them back. Each and every one. That is all we do really…

Haiku is at its most sublime when its tangible details are tinged by the Intangible, the visible breathing through the Invisible.

Let's reveal a secret! Why is it that we can consider all true haiku to be sacred and sublime?

A disciple of **Ramana Maharshi** lost his son and in his anguish came to the blessed sage and asked, 'What is God?' The sage saw that the answer was concealed in the question. His reply? 'What is … is God.'

And so, our interpenetration with all phenomena consists of this incredible immensity!

Finally, **Li Bai** knew all about disappearing. He describes it, succinctly:

> Birds vanishing in the sky, the last cloud fades,
> Sitting together, the mountain and I . . .
> Now only the mountain remains

Li Bai

Simple, isn't it?

Haiku Enlightenment

WRITING HAIKU: USEFUL TIPS

Dedication is the first tip, after which come more mundane matters. In a letter to a friend, **Bashō** says:

> 'I've worn out my body in journeys that are as aimless as the winds and clouds, and expended my feelings on flowers and birds. But somehow I've been able to make a living this way, and so in the end, unskilled and talentless as I am, I give myself wholly to this one concern, poetry…'

> (*From the Country of Eight Islands*, Columbia University Press, 1960)

•   Always have a notebook in your pocket – you never know when the haiku moment is going to manifest itself. A pencil for notes, say, and a pen for your first draft. As was noted in the beginning of this book, we do not seize Reality: Reality seizes us. Be prepared! Also, be prepared for weeks or months when nothing happens, when there are no haiku.

•   Keep your eyes and your ears open – but not too intently, not fanatically! Look! Listen! Strike while the iron is hot!

Or you'll miss it.

> the pond mirrors
> a flying squirrel
> over the wisteria
>
> **Kikaku**

One second too soon, one second too late – no haiku moment!

Have all the senses at the ready. On the haiku path, if your sight doesn't actually improve, your percipience will. You will notice new things in a new way:

231

look at his face . . .
> the cricket!
> such determination!

Yamaguchi Syuson

- As in the above haiku, you might prefer to avoid using capital letters except, perhaps, for the first word. Note also that titles are not used for individual haiku but a sequence, or *rensaku*, may be named if we wish to identify the locus of the haiku.

- Revise at leisure. Be ruthless! When your notebook is full, select the very best haiku and write them out again, carefully, in a fancier notebook. Keep copies on your PC, if you use one. Now, which ones *are* the best? Those moments of pure awareness, not created or imagined by you; moments of grace that happened to you in intimate commune with nature. Again, you cannot go wrong if you listen to the advice of **Bashō**. Imbibe every word: 'Your poetry issues of its own accord when you and the object have become one – when you have plunged deep enough into the object to see something like a hidden glimmering there...' And again: 'Submerge yourself into the object until its intrinsic nature becomes apparent, stimulating poetic impulse...' There are hundreds of haikuists who ignore this advice and their work suffers as a consequence, lacking in depth, spontaneity, atmosphere and resonance. If you remember nothing else, you have more than enough in this to succeed.

- Try writing a haiku sequence – a particular place at a particular time of the year. It will concentrate the mind on the notion of a thematic unity and diversity that exists within any given season and locale, the everyday miracles waiting for your contemplation. Nothing should be beneath you. (Or above you). On the haiku path, nothing is trite if conceived in the haiku moment.

- Keep your haiku in the present tense. The haiku moment is here and now – though it may be coloured by our past lives and memories, even by dreams and fantasies. Of course, once you have mastered this all-important rule – but only then – are you to write the occasional fictional haiku, such as the one by **Buson** given earlier when he steps on his dead wife's comb. It's a classic, never mind that his wife outlived him!

- Avoid the use of "I" and "me" and "mine" as much as possible. When the interior and exterior landscapes merge as one – enlightenment – there is little room for the "I".

- The three-line, 5-7-5 configuration is a good discipline for beginners. You may wish to stick with it. In time, however, you may be more at home with the free-style haiku of a dozen or so syllables.

- Read your haiku aloud, over and over again. If the rhythm is not natural, try varying the lines. Maybe line 3 should be line 1 or vice versa? It often happens that a haiku sounds best if the second line is the longest of the three, followed by a break (such as a dash) and a lift in the third line. The pause (after the first, or second, line) is called a *kire* and may be denoted by ellipsis (three dots), a dash, a comma or a colon. The word 'caesura', meaning a pause in verse, means to 'cut off'. You will also see haiku in this book, and elsewhere, which discard punctuation when the caesura is deemed obvious. Discarding punctuation can sometimes lead to an engaging ambiguity.

- Try to eliminate connective tissue, words such as "like" or the definite and indefinite articles – "the" and "a" – without going overboard or being cryptically telegrammatic. Be sparing with adjectives and adverbs. Listen to your haiku – if it contains two or more words ending in "ing", for instance, then some surgery may be needed.

- When is a haiku finished? How long does the haiku moment last? Interesting questions? Maybe this haiku answers them:

> a camellia fell;
> a cock crowed;
> some more flowers fell

Baishitsu

- Haiku is a spiritual path. Without the spiritual dimension, the cultivation of haiku may become frivolous or dilettantish. Much of it was hollow before **Bashō** arrived on the scene. When the spirit is alive in the haiku moment, resonances can be intuited, without the use of simile, as in **Bashō's**:

> lightning flashes
> and a night heron's squawk
> shoots into darkness

Bashō

See the note on *toriawase* in the Glossary. Try to find haiku in this book, or in any other, which contain *toriawase* or any of the other qualities explained in the Glossary. This will help your attentiveness as a reader of haiku, your own and others. Curiously enough, the example of *toriawase* given in the Glossary has lightning in it as well. Remember, with or without *toriawase*, a good haiku retains a mystery and a freshness for all time. Go through this book again and see if some haiku have a different impact on you at a second or third reading.

- If you do not have a formal spiritual practice such as chanting, meditation, tai chi or prayer, being alone with Nature is enough. Contemplate trees, grasses, the sky – let go, enter, intermingle with creation. Lose the head! Look at what happened to **D. E. Harding**: 'What actually happened was something absurdly simple and unspectacular: I stopped thinking. A peculiar quiet, an odd kind of alert limpness or numbness, came over me. Reason and imagination and all mental chatter died down... Past and future dropped away. I forgot who and what I was, my name, manhood, animalhood, all that could be called mine. It was as if I had been born that instant, brand new, mindless, innocent of all memories. There existed only the Now, that present moment and what was clearly given in it. To look was enough'. (*On Having No Head*, 1961) And so it should be with us.

- Use plain language. Anglo-Saxon words (if you write in English) tend to be more concrete and simpler than their Latinate brothers and sisters.

- Occasional internal rhyme or half-rhyme is fine but end rhyme is usually inappropriate.

- If you are lucky enough to have a garden – with a pond – find out what you should plant to attract interesting visitors throughout the year. Buddleia for butterflies, for instance, berries for birds. Plan your garden so that there is something to enliven the senses all year round. Relax in your garden with a good book, say *A Haiku Garden* by **Stephen Addis** (Weatherhill, 1996) or *A haiku menagerie* by the same author (Weatherhill 1992), with their respective themes of flora and fauna, culled from Japanese classics.

- Increase your nature vocabulary in as many realms as possible – birds, insects, plants, animals, rocks, the weather and so on. From time to time, try to use a *kigo* or season word that is associated with your country or region.

- Read the haiku classics, over and over again, and read the best of the moderns, such as **Santōka**. Cultivate reverence in your haiku work and seek out silence. Remember, each one of us is unique and we all find ourselves, daily, in unique situations. Be brave enough to express your own visions and the textures of life as you apprehend them. Haiku is about everything and nothing:

> a gleam of lightning!
>> the sound of rain
>>> dripping through bamboos

Buson

- Enjoy yourself!

> nearly sixty . . .
> with childhood glee, cycling
> through the evening snow

Keith J. Coleman
(*Blithe Spirit*, June 2009)

This has the quality of *akarusa*, bright cheeriness.

T
H
I
N
K

The bargain that intuition seems to drive is that it will serve you if you serve it. You must obey your intuition to cultivate it, to develop it, and to retain the use of it. This is a voluntary act. In colloquial language, you have a hunch, and the hunch is an involuntary experience. Whether or not you obey it is up to you. If it is a real hunch, an intuition, you will inevitably regret it if you do not. These experiences will increase in frequency if you obey them, and if you don't they will cease altogether.

— **Joseph Sadony**

A
B
O
U
T

I
T

- Celebrate aspects of your own culture and topography. Look for found haiku or hidden haiku in your favourite writers of prose and poetry. Sometimes a little editing helps:

leafy island . . .
>flapping herons wake
>>the drowsy water rats

>>**Yeats**
>>(culled from *The Stolen Child*)

- Cultivate sentiment, avoid sentimentality. Remind yourself to be passively aware, each waking hour of the day, and use as many of your senses as you can. The over-active brain may come between you and the haiku moment. From time to time, consciously avoid overstimulation. Try pacifying the mind, naturally. Drink green tea or herbal fusions that have been tried and tested in your clime.

- If you have a second or third language at your command, write translations or versions of haiku that have impressed you. This will cultivate your haiku style and sensibility. Try translating some of your own haiku as well: this could lead to a back-translation – revising the original.

- Keep a very open mind! Haiku possibilities are everywhere. The haiku spirit is limitless:

autumn wind
>everything visible
>>is haiku

>>**Kyoshi**

- Submit previously unpublished haiku, or haiku in translation, to a haiku journal or poetry magazine. Subscribe to one or two journals such as *Frogpond* (USA) *Modern Haiku* (USA) or *Blithe Spirit* (UK). Explore haiku links on the Internet, such as *haikuworld*, and learn to enjoy the beauty of *haiga* (illustrated haiku). Avoid overdose. Read and re-read the classics but not too many at a time. Sign up to receive a *Daily Issa*[5] email. Check haiku archives and resources, such as the Haiku Foundation.

---

[5] *Haiku of Kobayashi Issa website, curated by David Lanoue*

- You have seen many beautiful haiku in this book, one hopes. However, it is well to ponder **J. W. Hackett's** advice: 'Remember that lifefulness, not beauty, is the real quality of haiku'. An extreme example of **Hackett's** dictum might be the following by **Nagata Koi** (1900 – 1997), a frightening haiku from his *A dream like this world* (Japan 2000, trs. Naruta Nana & Mitsutani Margaret):

> an old cat, straining, shits—
> in such a pose
> my mother dies in winter
>
> **Nagata Koi**

Repulsive? It might be best to forget haiku if your inclinations tend towards mere prettification or chocolate-box imagery. Take up flower arrangement instead! (Though this, too, is a rigorous path when properly pursued). Ultimately, haiku is about fearless engagement with life and death, a close encounter with the world and shorn of illusion. It's about being more honest than you ever thought possible. Honest, yes, but not dourly serious all the time. Light touches of self-effacing humour are perfectly acceptable as in **Issa's**

> like some of us
> he looks rather important—
> this snail
>
> **Issa**

Every day is a good day.

—**Ummon**

Haiku Enlightenment

GLOSSARY OF USEFUL TERMS

It is not necessary to be familiar with all of these terms but, in themselves, they are pointers towards certain qualities or potentialities worth looking out for when reading haiku, *senryu* and *renku* (or *renga*, linked verse) or when revising one's own work.

Ada: a mood in haiku suggesting child-like innocence, a propensity to be surprised

Akarusa: cheery brightness

Ari no mama: recognizing things as they are, being as one is

Aware: a feeling in haiku of the impermanence of phenomena – in the midst of life we are in death

Buddhism: the teachings and culture of Gautama the Buddha

Butsuga ichinyo: identification of haiku poet with the subject of haiku

Chinsei: Tranquillity. In his Preface to *Lyrical Ballads*, **Wordsworth** says: 'Poetry is the spontaneous overflow of powerful feelings: it takes its origin from emotion recollected in tranquillity'. The haikuist can often do without recollection, finding tranquillity in the scene before us, here and now, as in this from **Buson**: pear blossoms – /reading a letter by moonlight/ a woman, **Ueda, Makoto**. *The path of flowering thorn: the life and poetry of Yosa Buson*, Stanford University Press, 1998.

Chiri: in season-word lists this covers the wide geography of mountains, rivers, hills etc.

Christianity: the teachings and culture of Jesus the Christ

Dubutsu: in season-word lists, this covers animals, birds and insects

Furyu: restrained elegance

Gendai: modern or avant-garde haiku

Ginko: a compositional stroll

Gyuji: the name in a season-list for holidays and festivals, Hallowe'en etc.

Haibun: prose written in a style which allows the inclusion of haiku, very often involving travel or pilgrimage

Haiga: illustrated haiku, often filling in details that might be missing from the actual haiku itself. Today it extends to non-traditional forms, such as photo-haiga with calligraphy or contemporary type. You can find haiga sites on the Internet

Haigo: a pen-name used by *haijin*. **Bashō** was the pen-name used by **Matsuo Munefusa** (1644-94). It means a banana tree, a type that doesn't bear fruit in Japan – plantain or coarse banana – and is often miserable-looking in wet, windy weather! *Bashō-an* was his hut, made of the plantain leaves.

Haii: the eternal spirit of haiku, found everywhere, especially in nature

Haijin: accomplished writer(s) or master(s) of haiku

Harae: cleansing, purification

Hisan: a word for pathos. Our haiku will be devoid of hisan if we do not develop compassion in our daily lives. **Santōka** tells us that 'anything that has not really taken place in someone's heart cannot be haiku poetry'.

Hogan-biiki: a natural sympathy for all that lives, especially the lowliest creatures and outcasts

Hokku: the opening stanza of a linked verse composition (*renku*) and the immediate antecedent of the modern haiku

Hon'i: the poetic essence of certain places

Honkadori: literary allusion, a haiku that echoes a previous well-known haiku, or part of it

Hosomi: understatement or modesty

Ichibutsu shitate: the quality of closely-focussed haiku, often centred on one object only

Jiku: a name in a season-word list for climatic and atmospheric

Jisei: death haiku, one-breath poems written with one's last breath

Kado: the Way of Poetry, thinking like a poet, feeling like a poet, being like a poet, through thick and thin

Kanjaku: serenity in desolation

Karumi: a lightness of touch in haiku style

Kensho: seeing into the true nature of things, clarity, enlightenment (see also *satori*)

Kidai: seasonal topic in haiku conditions

Kigo: a word or expression used to evoke a particular season. A *kigo* conveys *kidai*.

Kire: a pause in haiku, after the first or second line, often indicated by a dash

Kireji: cutting word in Japanese haiku to indicate the *kire* or caesura.

Glossary

Koan: Zen-Buddhist riddle

Koga: classical grace, often influenced by Chinese aesthetics. It's not a bad idea for haikuists to read the T'ang Dynasty poets, for instance, as well as the classics of their own culture

Kukai: a meeting of haiku poets, following a *ginko*

Kyoku: crazy verse, once a term for haiku

Makoto: appealing honesty, openness in haiku

Mononoke: nature spirits or nature energy

Mujō: impermanence, transience

Muyō: emptiness, uselessness, an idle awareness open to the present moment

Muyōsha: a useless person, not overly distracted by activity (see *muyō*)

Nioi: interpenetration of fragrances

Renku: also called *renga*. Linked verse, from the 14th.century, or earlier, to the present day, often composed at *renku* parties, with a distinguished poet giving the *hokku*, setting the tone or season and out of which subsequent verses evolve. The couplet (7-7 syllables) following the three-line *hokku* is the *wakiku*

Rensaku: a sequence of haiku written more or less around the same time and place

Sabi: loneliness in haiku, quiet elegance, undefined longing

Saijiki: a dictionary of season words. An international *saijiki* was published in **William J. Higginson's** *The Haiku Seasons: poetry of the natural world* (Kodansha International, 1996). Over 600 seasonal themes are covered in his *Haiku World: an international poetry almanac* (Kodansha International, 1996)

Satori: flash of enlightenment, liberation of consciousness from its normal day-to-day structuring of reality

Seikatsu: in season-word lists, this covers ordinary, traditional human activity portrayed in senryu and haiku – blackberry picking, seaweed gathering, for example

Senryu: a lighter form of haiku, concentrating more on people than on nature

Shasei: sketching from nature, the immediate scene. This was the style and method advocated by the 20th century master, **Shiki Masoaka**

Shibumi: beauty found in undramatic images, the half-hidden, toned down

Shikan: a meditative state achieved effortlessly by those on the haiku path

Shinto: traditional Japanese belief system, involving the spirits of Nature and ancestor worship. (Shintoists have shrines, Buddhists have temples)

Shiori: loneliness in haiku coupled with an acceptance of fate or note of ambiguity

Shokubutsu: in season-word lists this covers all types of plants peculiar to your own environment

Sono mama: factual observation of natural phenomena without any emotional adornment

Teijū hyōhaku: settled wandering

Tenmon: in season-word lists this covers meteorological observations, i.e. the weather and the appearance of heavenly bodies

Toriawase: seemingly disconnected phenomena perceived by one or more of the senses in a haiku moment, unified in a strange resonance. A term with a similar meaning is *renso*: a flash/of lightning, the sound of dew/falling from a bamboo. (**Buson**)

Ukiyo: this term is used to describe the impermanence and fragility of our mortal lives: *das Leben ein Traum*, life is a dream

Unsui: literally "cloud and water," a monk on pilgrimage to find insight or a teacher

Uta-makura: a so-called 'poetic pillow'; certain geographical areas that have inspired countless haiku

Wabi: beauty found in austerity

Yugen: a quality of depth and mystery. Hidden beauty. This elegance and other qualities may emerge unbidden in our work as we grow older and wiser with haiku!

Yukon: virility, whether in men or animals

Zappai: superficial *senryu* or pseudo-haiku of no literary merit or spiritual content.

Zen: a Japanese development of Chan, Chinese Buddhism

Zenkan: pure perception

Zôka: the indivisible essence of all things which is known to the haikuist in sublime moments.

INDEX OF POEMS

A Note About the Translations

All poems are rendered into English (and sometimes Irish) by the author, unless otherwise indicated. Irish, German, and Spanish language poems are direct translations; others are English language versions by the author.

INDEX

247

Haiku Enlightenment

ABOUT THE AUTHOR

Gabriel Rosenstock was born in postcolonial Ireland and is a bilingual writer with a strong preference for writing in the Irish language. Poet, haikuist, tankaist, novelist, author-translator of over 200 books, including books for children, he is also an essayist, short story writer, playwright and 'champion of forlorn causes' (the phrase is Hugh MacDiarmid's). He is a member of Aosdána (the Irish Academy of Arts and Letters), former chairman of Poetry Ireland/Éigse Éireann, on the Board of Advisors to Poetry India, Irish-language advisor for the poetry journal *THE SHOp*, and a Foundation Associate of The Haiku Foundation. Gabriel and his wife, Eithne Ní Chléirigh, have four children, Héilean, Saffron, Tristan and Éabha and oodles of haiku-loving grandchildren.

Made in the USA
Middletown, DE
27 February 2020